The Art of Cosmic Creation

By Lavender Moon

Channeled through Amber Tawn

Copyright © 2020 Amber Tawn

All rights reserved. No part of this book may be used or reproduced in any manner whatsoever, including Internet usage, without permission from Amber Tawn, except in the case of brief quotations used for reviews or critical articles.

For information about Amber's YouTube channel and podcast, visit www.ambertawn.com

Book design, photographs, and illustrations by Amber Tawn. Edited by Sandra Watts

This book is only intended for informational, entertainment, and educational purposes. The material in this book is not intended as medical, psychological, psychiatric, financial, or legal advice. For such advice, consult a qualified professional. The author assumes no legal liability for any damages, losses, or other consequences of any decisions, or actions, subsequent to, or based on, the material in this book.

DEDICATION

This book is dedicated to YOU.

I stand in awe of your expansive being. Always trust your SELF and know that you are never alone.

ACKNOWLEDGMENTS

First and foremost, I want to thank my grandpa, Abe. No matter where I was, or what I was doing, I never forgot you for even one moment. You are forever a part of me. You taught me to look for those things that are easily overlooked and to listen for the sounds that often go unheard. Without you I would have missed my greatest gift. I love you forever and ever. I thank my "Gramsbear", Henny, my biggest cheerleader, my heart, and the one who taught me to always trust myself. You gave me so much love and I love you forever.

I want to thank my mother, Cindy, I am here because of you and without you, I would never be who I am. You taught me to be fierce, to never back down and to never give up, you lead by example, I love you infinity.

I want to thank my brother, Louis for being my partner in crime and for helping me to record the messages of Lavender Moon. You may have not been able to understand my work, but you always supported everything I did. The years we spent together playing with our imaginations truly paved the way for this book. You translate through music, and I through words, you are the Hierophant and I the Hermit; we are eternally two sides of the same coin.

I want to thank my father, David, who led me on the path of meditation, eternal self-inquiry and inner exploration. I get my channeling abilities from you and I love you always my "dadillac", (yes that's a play on Cadillac for everyone reading this!).

A very special thank you to Sierra Bender, author of

Goddess to the Core: An Inspired Workout to Maximize Your Fitness, Beauty & Power, my spiritual mentor, "big sister", and the one who helped me to find my medicine. You impacted my life more than you could ever know.

I thank my wonderful husband, Krishan who has psychic gifts of his own. Your patience and help made this book possible.

I would like to thank all of my AMAZING YouTube subscribers who have been with me on this journey. Without you and your support, this book could not exist. Through interacting with you all, I have found myself and I am forever grateful to all of you. A special thank you Psyche, you've been there since the beginning.

A special thank you to Julianne Victoria, for all of your guidance on publishing and for your friendship.

A special thank you to my editor, Sandra Watts. You not only edited my work but believed in it as well, I will be forever grateful for all of your support.

Finally, thank you to my beautiful son Avi and my "fur-daughter", Saffie. You love me everyday and I love you forever and ever to infinity and beyond.

NOTE TO READER

"When you wish upon a star, makes no difference who you are. Anything your heart desires, will come to you…"

~Leigh Harline & Ned Washington for Walt Disney's 1940 adaptation of Pinocchio

Dearest Reader,

Walt Disney was a master of **The Art of Cosmic Creation**, and this little song truly sums up the message that is at the heart of this book. Walt Disney was a human whose influence is still felt today and will continue to be experienced by many generations after us. His vision was so great that it has taken on a life of its own and infused our modern culture with its presence.

We will call the soul's ability to express its true nature through the vehicle of physical reality **radiance**, and Walt Disney had great radiance. He had a dream and a vision that he was passionate about. He allowed his desire to create cartoons to saturate his entire being and, ultimately, his entire reality. He became one with his desire and brought happiness to many generations with his gift of contribution.

The Art of Cosmic Creation is the process by which you can live a fully expressed life by embracing your purpose and allowing it to blossom and infuse your reality with your soul's brilliant radiance. This book will teach you how to change your life by essentially shaping your reality to allow for the multidimensional expansion of your essence.

Lots of Love to you on your journey,
Amber Tawn

Contents

DEDICATION iii

ACKNOWLEDGMENTS iv

NOTE TO READER vi

INTRODUCTION..1

1 THE WHEEL 9

2 THE HAUNTED HOUSE 30

3 LIONS IN THE DARK..43

4 COLUMBIA 65

5 THE PARTY..77

6 THE SPIRITUAL MOUTH...97

7 THE SACRED TRIANGLE OF CREATION: THE PUSH AND PULL OF DESIRE..126

8 WITH ACTION COMES ATTRACTION 151

9 THE ART OF COSMIC CREATION...165

10 A VISION FOR THE FUTURE 174

ABOUT THE AUTHOR 178

"Stars are an entry point or a gateway from the subtle, energetic realm into the physical"

~ Lavender Moon

INTRODUCTION
A STAR IS BORN

Before we begin **The Art of Cosmic Creation**, it is necessary first to become comfortable with the terms and concepts that I will use throughout this book, as they will most likely be new to you. Please read through the entire introduction and do not skip over any part of it.

It is also necessary to explain how I came upon these terms and material for this book. I don't view this book as mine; really, it's more of a series of messages that I have "translated" from a non-physical consciousness, that I call "Lavender Moon", (more about that later after the explanation).

Let's begin with the concept of a "star" from Walt Disney's song because it will serve as a metaphor, and an example of how our own essence can create "something out of nothing". No one really knows how the universe came into being. However, the process of ongoing creation can still be witnessed today through a process known as **stellar nucleo-synthesis**, which takes place within the center of the celestial bodies we call stars. Through an orchestrated dance of attraction or gravity and intense pressure, heat, and light, the entire periodic table of elements that make up everything we know are birthed into being. Let us now move away from the technical terms of nuclear fusion and see these stellar giants for what they really are, masters of The Art of Cosmic Creation.

Stars are an entry point or a gateway from the subtle, energetic realm into the physical. Like the womb of a woman's body, it is a place where energy transforms into physical matter, and you are such a place as well. You are an expansive, multidimensional being who has the capability of shaping and transforming energy into matter. Like stars, we can essentially create "ex nihilo" or something out of nothing. Before you can do this, however, it's time to awaken to your truest form and become conscious of who and what you really are.

The consciousness or intention behind all creation, we will refer to as the **Source**. The Source Consciousness is so expansive that our human brains cannot begin to fathom its structure or limits. Because it doesn't seem to have any limits, I will also refer to the Source as the **Infinite**. Being human myself and currently limited by a physical human brain, I can only describe the process by which we exist individually, as a "filtering down" of Source Consciousness. There are many levels to this "filtering down", but I will only describe the most essential.

You are a massive, expansive, and multidimensional being, much like a star, whose purpose is to carry out the expression/expansion of the Infinite, by expressing and reflecting your unique, individual essence through physical reality. We each have something called the **Guiding Self**. The Guiding Self is like a small pooling of the Infinite (of which there are uncountable pools), although I see it as a vast ocean. The Guiding Self is a collective consciousness and your direct link to Source because it is a small droplet of the Infinite.

On the other end of the spectrum, we have the **partial self**, or the part of our being that streams into physical reality straight from the Guiding Self. Many of us are connected or filter down from the same Guiding Self but become "separate" in our physical vehicles. This "separation" and its purpose will be explained later. The Guiding Self is always providing you with direction whether you know it or not, and it is through communication with the Guiding Self that we consciously co-create our physical reality.

Over the pages that follow, I, Amber, engage in a conversation with a being who revealed itself to me in the form of an orb, or a ball of white light containing all the colors of the rainbow. You don't have to take my word or my description for it, because I asked this being for a photo that I could use as proof to show everyone when I deliver the messages and this being agreed. This is a photograph of the being that I call Lavender Moon, which can also be found on the cover of this book.

I call Lavender Moon a being in the singular, but it's really a collective consciousness. As you will come to understand in detail, our "separateness" is only an illusion. Our level of consciousness and state of awareness provides the lens through which we perceive ourselves. We are all one consciousness here on earth, but due to our current state of awareness, we see ourselves as separate individuals (and you will find out why as you read further).

This collective consciousness that I call Lavender Moon has evolved past this individual perception, and instead communicates and operates as a sort of hive consciousness. This is the only way that I can describe it to you. You can think of Lavender Moon as a civilization that is older than humanity. I don't have the exact numbers, but maybe over a millennia, being farther down the road in technology and understanding of the universe around us. For them, there is no separation between spiritual and scientific understanding.

This collective has been with us since our beginnings here on earth. They tell me that humanity is important to them because ultimately, we are all cosmically ONE. It is our growth in consciousness and understanding of ourselves and, ultimately, the universe that they are concerned with. They tell me that because we are all connected, the more we grow and express ourselves here on earth, the more consciousness expands everywhere throughout the universe.

I'm also not the only one writing these messages. There's nothing new here, just that I can break things down through my own understanding; in a way that makes this information digestible. They tell me that they have been sending messages to humanity for a very long time. It is through our lens of awareness and understanding that we have interpreted these messages.

Lavender Moon tells me that because we are experiencing a collective shift of consciousness here on earth as we move into the Age of Aquarius, these messages require an update in our latest language and understanding. I have done my best to understand, "translate", and convey these messages to you, the reader, as best as possible. These messages were transferred to me telepathically through some frequency-based technology that I don't have the capacity to describe. I hope that my translation of the thoughts conveys these messages to you as intended by Lavender Moon.

I hand wrote all of these messages over a period of six months. I managed to wake up at 4:00 am most days, to receive and write the messages before my workday began. Although you only see the answers, this work was more like a dialogue. Whenever Lavender Moon described a concept to me, I asked the questions: "What does this mean? What does this look like? How can I describe this? How can we apply this to our daily lives?" The result is this book, the pictures that I drew (which they gave me in order, to understand these complex concepts), and the exercises that you will find at the end of each chapter so that you can apply these ideas to your daily life.

I have personally practiced every exercise in this book, and I can tell you that life is very different for me than it was two years ago. I now have a sense of purpose, direction, and focus that I never had before. I experience the magic of life and honestly feel a direct connection to something much larger than myself. I wish this for you, too, if this is what you are looking for.

I have written all of the lessons and instructions given to me, in the exact order that they were given. It's critical that you read every chapter and practice every exercise in the exact order in which they are presented. Lavender Moon has made it clear that this order is important for understanding, and I can't stress this enough. The messages are organized in such a way that they work on both the conscious and subconscious levels. I'm not really able to explain the process, but this is what was told to me.

I was given five important dreams throughout my life, starting at age 16. Luckily I wrote each dream down the day after I had them. Little did I know that these dreams would culminate in this book. Lavender Moon explained that these dreams were meant not only for me but also for **YOU** as they contain the foundation for these messages. As you read these dreams, picture everything I say and describe in your mind's eye; by doing this, you will have had the dream as well, and these subconscious messages will be passed on to you.

I was also instructed to write these dreams in the present tense for this same reason. Lavender Moon was very specific on that. There's something about the tense that moves you into the experience and allows it to become your own. There are also certain messages and information conveyed visually, when you look at the image of Lavender Moon on the cover, which is why they allowed me to take this photo.

Lavender Moon has informed me that it is time to know and understand that this universe is multidimensional. They want us to be aware of their presence because it helps us to understand and open to the multidimensionality of this universe. Every word in this book also carries with it multidimensional meaning. To make the best use of this book, I encourage you to mark it up, highlight, and write down notes of thoughts and ideas or messages that come to you as you read and complete the exercises. This book is meant to be interactive and transform into a living document as you begin writing down your own messages.

The communication that I received is hard to describe, but when I "channel", it's like I become one with this collective consciousness, and there is no differentiation, although I have tried to differentiate with *italics*. When you read through my dreams and personal experiences, they will be in italics to differentiate them from the messages of Lavender Moon. In addition, all of the new terms that we mentioned will be **in bold,** defined and explained in a certain order. You will also notice a lot of repetition throughout the messages, and that repetition has a purpose as well.

I hope that this book is helpful to you in your life as it was, is, and will continue to be in mine. I hope that this book serves as a constant companion that will bring you connection, direction, and the conviction to always trust your unique inner light. Know that you are never alone and that "separateness" is only an illusion.

I take every word in this book very seriously, because many beings went through a lot of trouble to reach through time and space to let us know that we are all worthy of living a fully self-expressed life simply because we EXIST.

Take these messages to heart and know that I wish you happiness, joy, peace, freedom, and love on your path. May all of your desires find complete expression in physical reality. It is through these messages that I have come to know the nature of our existence and The Art of Cosmic Creation. Now, let us now begin instruction…

"Our level of consciousness and state of awareness provides the lens through which we perceive ourselves"

~Lavender Moon

1 THE WHEEL
EVERYTHING IS VIBRATION

In a dream...

I find myself on an endless beach. The sky is awash with pink, peach, orange, blue, and purple. The crystalline colors reflect off of the sand, creating a sparkling, shimmering, prismatic effect. It seems like the beach where I live, except I can't see any houses, people, animals, or the ocean. Amidst the unusual stillness, I feel like the only person on earth.

Suddenly, I become aware of a warm wind, or is it? It feels almost alive with breath. It begins to blow all around me, no... through me. "Can this be possible?" I ask myself. It feels as if it's touching every cell of my being, and in response, every atom of my being begins to dance, to vibrate at such a rate that I'm hardly sure I'm still there at all. Then somehow, it's so still and so silent, and simultaneously, I feel everything humming and moving through me and I, through everything.

Now a strange sensation begins to blossom in my heart, is my heart still there? I feel an intense pulsating energy, and my heart opens. It feels like an intense bass speaker playing into my chest, and I begin to bend backward automatically. Although I feel no pain or physical sensation, I suddenly feel afraid. And I FEEL a voice say, "Don't be afraid, let go, open your heart." I'm not sure how I understand the voice because I don't hear it with my ears exactly. I begin to move into what I can only describe as a "wheel pose" in yoga. I do not have a body, and yet, I do.

I feel no pain, no stretch; all I can feel is vibration and the warm wind blowing through me, and everywhere around me. Then, suddenly, I'm not alone. I feel the presence of millions and billions of beings all lovingly pulsating with me, and together we become a cosmic symphony. I can no longer tell the difference between sky, land, up, down, me, them. We all blend into one another, and I know the truth, everything is vibration, everything is of one substance, one Source, we are all one, and we are never alone.

I was 16 years old when I had this dream. I didn't know it at the time, but it was my first direct experience with the Guiding Self. I would not, however, understand the true significance of this dream until I was 37 years old. I remember waking up and not knowing who I was for a few moments. I just lay there, still feeling my body humming with a deep sense of peace and unconditional love. In this dream, I was shown the true substance of creation, something we can only understand with our human intellect as vibration.

Vibration is the movement and continual expansion of consciousness. Vibration is the oscillation of Source substance or consciousness, constantly seeking new levels of awareness through expression. It is the clay the Infinite uses to create, and it is the substance that we will learn how to consciously shape and mold as an expression of our essence or our soul. We are an expression of the Infinite, a seed desiring and holding the potential to become an oak.

We possess the ability to harness and direct consciousness. We can use consciousness to mold and shape physical reality as a unique expression of our essence. A star forms matter through intense pressure and intense heat. In the same way, we can create by focusing our thoughts (pressure) in the direction of our desire (heat). We are stars in our own right, suns around which our individual universe revolves. The universe is reflected through us. We reflect and express the Infinite.

The 5 Domains of Physical Reality

The 5 Domains of Physical Reality are your domains of self expression. You are sovereign, reigning over each domain and shaping them into reflections of your soul.

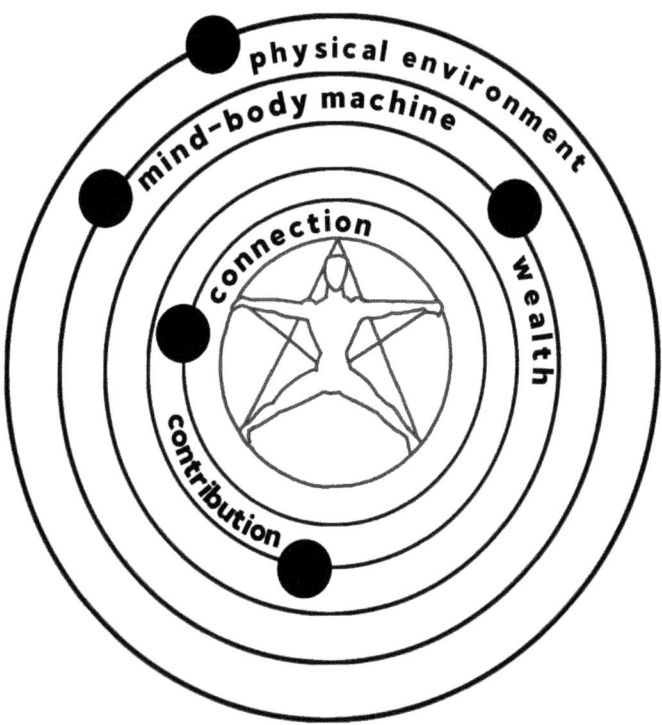

"The universe is reflected through us. We REFLECT and EXPRESS the Infinite"
- Lavender Moon

Let us now discuss the term "desire" and how desire can be consciously harnessed, to guide and shape your life. The word "desire" comes from the Latin, [de sidere], which means: "from the stars". As we have learned, stars are the gateways that connect the energetic and physical realms. They are furnaces that create the clay or the building blocks of reality. We want you to imagine the Guiding Self, your spirit, or your true essence as a star. Desire is a message and direct communication from your spirit. We define **desire** as your soul's blueprint for evolution.

Desire can be imagined as a set of coordinates in the form of a series of frequencies or thought waves, much like musical notes that act as a cosmic combination or key. This key unlocks the creative potentiality of the collective consciousness we call the Guiding Self. If you think of the traditional shape of a star or starfish with five rays, you can imagine the Guiding Self as the center or nucleus. From that pool of consciousness, it seeks and desires to expand outward or **radiate**. As our awareness increases, we radiate outward and emit rays of light. The light can be seen as a metaphor for increased awareness or expansion of consciousness. As this light shines, the light, or awareness, in turn, causes consciousness to expand all around us. Just as Walt Disney has probably touched your life somehow, so can your light flow into everything and everyone around you.

There are **five domains of physical reality** through which we project our essence. These domains are five paths through which you can expand your awareness. Imagine your soul as sovereign. These domains are where you hold dominion or "divine rule". You can influence these domains and shape them as an expression of your soul. In this scenario, you are the artist, and you will use the clay chosen by you (the life circumstances that you were born into) to shape a masterpiece. These five domains are your **Physical Environment**, **Mind-Body Machine**, **Wealth**, **Contribution**, and **Connection**.

Physical Environment: This is where you live: the room, apartment or house, and ultimately the town or city where you reside.

Mind-Body Machine: This is your body, which contains your brain and your thoughts. It is the place where you can contribute to or take away from your physical/mental health and comfort. We call this the "mind-body machine" because it is the vehicle your spirit uses to navigate this reality, like an avatar.

Wealth: This is your money and anything else that contributes to your wealth. In this current system of reality, wealth is necessary and can appear in many different forms. It is your way of sustaining yourself and supporting the lifestyle or reality needed to meet your desires.

Contribution: This is the area of your life where you can contribute your feelings and ideas to the world around you. We call this the area of "contribution" instead of "career" because its function changes from childhood to adulthood. In our early years, it's our ability to express our ideas and views to others and receive validation (or not) at home. Then it shifts into school as you engage with academic material and peers. This domain's development culminates in your career. We want you to see "career" as the venue you will use to contribute to and help expand the awareness of consciousness to benefit all in a way that is unique to your soul.

Connection: This is the area of relationships of all kinds: familial, romantic, and platonic. This domain represents

HOW you connect to others, including how you connect to yourself and to the divine.

The Guiding Self and the Expansion of Consciousness

As your awareness increases your consciousness radiates outward and emits rays of light that add to the awareness and expansion of all creation.

True power is the ability to allow the fullness of you to radiate outward into each of these five domains of physical reality. In other words, the soul seeks to express itself through each of these five areas. We seek to mold each domain into an expression of our soul. The purpose of this life is to infuse physical reality with your unique essence.

Recap:

Desire is the message we receive from our soul. Our soul is inextricably linked to the Infinite or the source of all consciousness. Think of your soul as a droplet in the vast ocean of infinite consciousness. These desires are your soul's blueprint for evolution and expansion of all consciousness. Through your desires, you will reach new levels of awareness and express potentials desiring to be in existence. Desires contain the instructions by which we can fully express ourselves through five domains of physical reality:

> **Physical Environment:** Our direct surrounding
> **Mind-body Machine:** How we feel in our bodies and how we take care of them
> **Wealth:** How we work with and manage our money
> **Contribution:** How we enrich society through our work or career
> **Connection:** How we connect and relate to others

The point of life is to express ourselves through each of these five domains and radiate our spirit outward into physical reality. When we do this, we add brilliance and higher levels of awareness to all creation.

We already create our reality, whether we know it or not, but the point is to learn how to do this consciously through increased awareness of who we truly are. Depression comes from unfulfilled potential. When we are being less than who we truly are, we enter a state where our energy or consciousness cannot expand, so it begins to slow down. We begin to vibrate at a slower rate. Think of your soul as a plant growing in a tiny pot with no room for its roots to expand. When this happens, the plant weakens, withers, and dies. It never reaches its fullest potential or innate glory.

When our rate of vibration slows down, we find ourselves in perpetual negativity. Our five domains of physical reality begin to feel more like prisons and less like what they are; venues and opportunities for self-expression. Your physical reality becomes like a neglected garden; it is forgotten, dying, rotting, choked with weeds, and drying up. The quality of your life here on earth is in direct proportion to your ability to radiate your desires or instructions for your fullest potential outward into physical reality.

Jealousy is an excellent indicator that you are in discord with the Guiding Self. Jealousy means that you are ignoring the messages and desires of your spirit. You do this out of a lack of awareness and not because there is something wrong with you or that you are incapable of such things. Your desire is your soul's blueprint for evolution. Jealousy is anger at the perceived inability to express your desire at the sight of someone else showing their potential in an area where you are not. There is nothing wrong or shameful about depression, anger, or jealousy because it's all information from the Guiding Self.

The Guiding Self is your most significant Spirit Guide. In other words, our spirit is the mediator between our partial self (the part of us located inside this body in physical reality), and the Infinite. If you want something in life, your spirit speaks to you. If you have felt jealous or depressed, your spirit speaks to you. It was only a lack of awareness that "separated" you from your spirit. You are in constant communication with your Guiding Self, whether you know it or not. We can bridge the line of communication by becoming aware of our unique coordinates, which exist at the heart of our desires.

Everyone has a unique combination or set of coordinates that act as directions for your fullest expression. These coordinates are at the core of your every desire. It is becoming conscious of these coordinates that will help you to shape your reality. What were you really looking for when you bought that new shirt? What were you really looking for when you entered into a relationship with that person? What were you really looking for when you decided to go on that very first interview? Understanding these coordinates will help you distinguish between the "wants" of the Ego and the "desires" of the Guiding Self.

Before we explore the difference between "want" and "desire," let us first find your coordinates. We will take you through an exercise that will give you the keys to unlock your potential by increasing your awareness of what you seek to express, by bringing your desires to fruition. We will then place your coordinates into something we call your **Guiding Star Compass** or **GSC**. Through each chapter, we will add information to your Guiding Star Compass. This infographic will serve as a tangible blueprint for your soul's path towards evolution, a pictorial representation of your soul's directions for experiencing and expressing what you came here to experience and express, how to expand your potential and consequently your awareness or consciousness.

Exercise 1: Finding Your Coordinates

Vibration is felt and not seen. In other words, vibration, like waves in an ocean, moves through us, and interacts with our consciousness. We feel or receive these vibrations and the information that they contain, and we experience them as feelings. It's not only important to know what you desire, but why you desire that thing or experience. You desire certain things in life because your essence contains certain seed vibrations that your consciousness seeks to expand and develop. Therefore, your soul is attracted to and seeks out experiences that contain a certain set of vibrations or coordinates that are the keys to your expansion.

Think of your soul once again as a seed planted in the soil of your physical reality. The vibrations contained inside of the physical things or experiences that you desire are the water, fertilizer, sunshine, carbon dioxide, and space you need to grow and develop into your greatest potential. As a result, you create beauty, shade, and oxygen all around you. You are looking for the FEELING something will give you, and NOT the physical object itself.

Let us now find out which feelings you are looking for, and which feelings or vibrations you seek to saturate your life with. This set of feelings or coordinates are how you will express your soul, they are instructions from the Creator, and we know this because you enjoy them and are attracted to them naturally. When you feel these feelings, you are in harmony or **resonance** with the Guiding Self. When you are not allowing yourself to pursue and have access to these feelings or vibrations, you are in **discord** with the Guiding Self.

Let us now begin to look at the five domains of physical reality through your imagination. Imagination is how you start to shape your reality because it is the projective part of your intuition. Premonition is the receptive part of the intuition where you receive impressions or information. In this physical reality, two forces are necessary for creation. These forces are "attraction" and "action". These forces work together like the Guiding Self and the partial self. Like a question and an answer, they are two parts of the same mechanism, working together to produce more possibilities. These forces work in tandem to increase the light of awareness amidst the darkness of ignorance.

In stars, the outward push of nuclear fusion (action), is balanced by the inward push of gravity (attraction). This balance keeps the star's form. In other words, the process of Cosmic Creation is accomplished by a balance of action and attraction as they work together focused by the heat of "desire" or the instructions from the Guiding Self.

Take your time with this exercise. You do not have to do it all in one sitting. Make sure you are in a place and time where you will not be disturbed. Do whatever you need to be in a calm state; play relaxing instrumental music, sit outside, or open a window. Then close your eyes and imagine your ideal physical environment, the house of your dreams.

If anything were possible, and you had no limitations, what type of home would you live in? Take your time and imagine the colors, the furniture, and the features. Now, imagine how you would feel in such a home. Get in touch with the adjectives that describe how you would feel in your ideal surroundings.

Would you feel more organized, cheerful, light, or enthusiastic? These feelings can be any adjectives that describe how you feel in these surroundings. What emotions or vibrations are stirred up inside you while "being in" and experiencing these surroundings?

Write down five feelings your ideal surrounding gives you. While picturing your dream home in your mind, use the sentence stem, "I feel..." to find your five vibrations.

Trust what comes to you because this is your Guiding Self giving you information. Are you open to hearing this information? Let go of all fear and doubt as you write what you feel.

Take these feelings and order them by importance. Which feelings are the most important? Which feelings ignite your imagination? Which feelings do you want to experience the most? Which do you need the most?

Allow number 1 to be the feeling you need the most and number 5, although important, you could do without if you had number 1.

Work your way through each domain, imagining your ideal body, and how you would feel in this body. Imagine your ideal amount of money to be making or saving or investing and all that you would do with it. Imagine the perfect career that would serve as a venue to express your talents, and imagine your ideal relationships with family, friends, and romantic partners. Write down each feeling and number it in order of importance. Next, place each number 1 from each domain into the rays of your Guiding Star Compass. These five "feelings" are what you are seeking to feel behind the physical.

The Guiding Star Compass

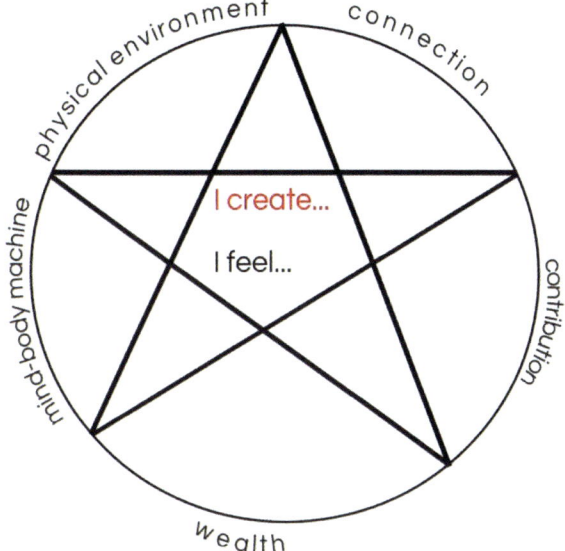

Finding Your Coordinates

How do you feel in your ideal physical environment?

1. I feel ......   2. I feel......   3. I feel......   4. I feel......   5. I feel......

How do you feel in your ideal physical body? (choose 5 feelings)

How do you feel in your ideal level of wealth? (choose 5 feelings)

How do you feel in your ideal career? (choose 5 feelings)

How do you feel in your ideal realtionships? (choose 5 feelings)

Order these feelings from 1-5, number 1 being your most desired feeling and number 5 being the feeling you would have as a result of having your most desired feeling (number 1).

Circle all of your number 1 feelings and list these 5 desired feelings. These 5 feelings are your coordinates, the feelings or vibrations you search for under physical choices. List them in any order into the rays of your Guiding Star Compass. Turn the 5 adjectives into 5 nouns to discover what you desire to create through physical reality. List these along the outside of the rays as shown in the example on the following page.

The Forces of ACTION and ATTRACTION within The Guiding Star Compass

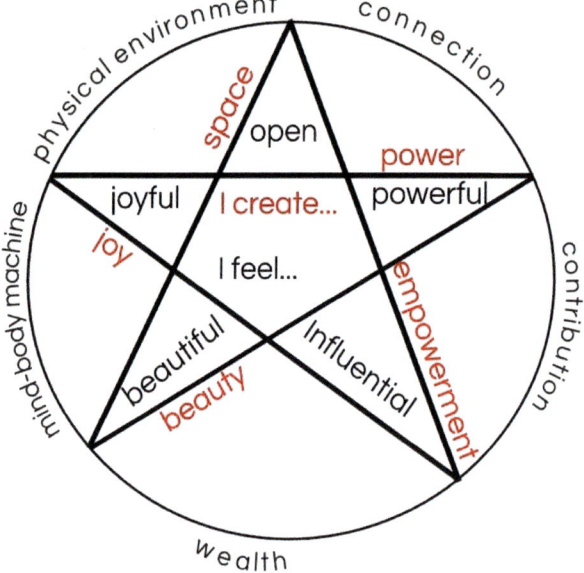

There are two forces: ACTION (in red) and ATTRACTION (in black). You want to attract each of your coordinates as well as project them outward. Turn each adjective into a noun to see what you want to create/give to this world.

The star symbolizes the soul's purpose of expression. As the soul grows in awareness, it grows in radiance. The circle symbolizes your space within the physical realm and the physical earth itself.

Troubleshooting:

How do you know that your number 1 is truly your number 1? Your number 1 will be the gateway to the other four. If you have number 1, it will open the door to your other four feelings, so in essence, you have all five. Also, what happens if a feeling repeats? What if the same adjective shows up for more than one domain? Then keep it only once and examine the number 2's. Which one is more important? Which one opens you up for the others?

In this exercise, you used your imagination as a tool to connect with your spirit, which is your vehicle for Cosmic Creation. Imagination is the active or the projective part of your intuition, while "perceiving what is to come" or "psychic impressions" are the passive/receptive part of the intuition. Everything has an active and passive, or receptive and projective nature, creating ebb and flow in the world of duality (physical reality). If you can imagine something, then it exists on an energetic level, and you can "draw it down" to you. When you imagine, you express a part of your unique perception into the creation and therefore create something unique and different. This is the purpose of "separation" between the Infinite, the Guiding Self, and the partial self; to produce infinite combinations and infinite possibilities. This separation, however, could not occur without the presence of Ego.

The Guiding Star Compass shows you the feelings and vibrations that the Guiding Self (your spirit as a fraction of the Infinite), is searching for behind the physical. This compass will help you to distinguish between the desires of the Guiding Self and the "wants" of the Ego. Remember that "desire" will bring about expansion and expression, while "want" will bring about possession and suffocation.

As you make daily choices, look over your compass and answer the following:

Will this choice (desire), expand/grow/increase my experience of_____(coordinate) through the five domains (the five kingdoms of my dominion)?

Will this desire expand/increase the vibration of_____(coordinate) and aid me in expressing_____(coordinate) through me/my life?

Will this desire cause me to radiate more_____(coordinate) into the world around me?

If the answers to these questions are yes, then this coordinate is a desire of the Guiding Self and not a "want" of the Ego.

Creation is composed of two opposing forces that lie on opposite ends of the spectrum: Integration and disintegration, formation and destruction. When we receive a desire, it is "from the stars", or from the cosmic womb of our soul, where something forms out of nothing (matter from vibration or consciousness). The purpose of desire is the expression of potential that is looking for awareness through expression. A desire leads to growth, expansion, and YOU, resonating at a higher frequency so that you can operate very closely to the Guiding Self while still remaining in physical reality. At this point, the partial self and the Guiding Self begin to resonate together in frequency or rate of oscillation and "dance" in the joy of perpetual creation and expression.

A "want" comes from the Ego, the part of the partial self that anchors itself into physical reality and creates the "veil" of separation. We need the Ego in order to remain in this physical body because it slows down our frequency enough to remain in this world of matter and duality. It is helpful to be aware of the Ego's purpose so that you do not get caught up in the "wants" of the Ego. There is a reason and purpose for duality, and you will see the interplay of polarity throughout these messages.

Let us now take a more in-depth look into **the continuum of duality**. When we enter into this physical world of action and reaction, a part of our consciousness (the partial self), must slow down in frequency or oscillation and remain at a certain rate in order to be anchored into the physical body, or mind-body machine. We would like you to imagine this as two points connected by a wave of vibration. On the top end of the spectrum, we find the Guiding Self as a fraction of the Infinite still located in the energetic-subtle realm. At the base of the spectrum, we find the partial self, anchored by the dense and slow-moving Ego that is all about limitation, definition, and structure because this is its function.

The Ego gives form to the formless; it is the vessel that contains the water. Notice how the waves stretch out and become slower as they enter the world of matter at the bottom. Although all points on the continuum are part of the same mechanism, this "slowing down of consciousness", through dimensions, creates a "duality" or a polarity. It creates a perceived (although not true) separation between the energetic and physical. Welcome to the "reality of duality". You are anchored here by the **"I"** and **"me"** of the Ego. This allows for infinite possibilities of expression, expansion, and growth.

As we collectively grow in our awareness, the time has come for us to reawaken to an expanded view of reality. It is time to enjoy our time in the **"I"** but to be aware that the **"I"** is an illusion and to operate from this new awareness. On the continuum of duality, we choose to move in either direction, towards expression or possession. Remember that your garden (your consciousness or spirit) is watered by the positive vibrations or coordinates you chose for your Guiding Star Compass. Your compass will help you to navigate your direction along the continuum. The Ego is a tool or trick your consciousness uses to anchor itself into physical reality. The Ego isn't your true essence. Desire is the vehicle that will take you upward, towards the Guiding Self.

"The Ego is the device through which the Infinite creates a temporary separation"

~Lavender Moon

2 THE HAUNTED HOUSE
LEAVE THE PRISON OF YOUR PAST BEHIND AND WALK OUT!

In a dream...

I know this place. It's the old Victorian home that I moved into when I was ten years old. There are so many bad memories here, my mother's alcoholism, fights, screaming, insomnia, and incessant paranormal experiences that terrified me. Although I left this place physically in 1992, here I am again, every night in my dreams, and it always ends the same way. I never escape; I never find a way out.

Even though I know this is the same house, it's dark and more chaotic with its never-ending crawl spaces. I'm lost, I'm scared, and I feel buried amidst the clutter of dusty old boxes filled with the junk of my past. No one lives here anymore, how did I get here? Why did I walk through the front door? Why did I come back? At the same time, I feel watched. In each room, I meet small trickster people, lost souls, and demons meaning me physical harm. I'm trying to get away, but I just can't, and I feel hopeless. I'm in front of my childhood bedroom at the top of the stairs that leads to the front door.

On this night, something different happens. The front door opens, and I see sunlight. An old man stands in the doorway, and I'm just frozen at the top of the stairs because it didn't quite compute that the door had actually opened. He waves his hands impatiently, "Come on!" he yells. Looking behind me, I see the dolls with their sharp teeth closing in on me, and I make a run for it, out the front door.

I made it! My heart is beating, and I can't believe that I made it out. Suddenly the terror arises as I remember that I'm being chased. As I'm about to turn around and look, the man grabs my arm and says, "Don't look back! Just keep walking". I question him, "But what about...". He then interrupts me mid-sentence and says in a stern voice, "I said DON'T look back!". For some reason, I trust him, and I understand beyond words, that if I don't look back or focus on it, I will withdraw my energy from there, and it will disappear.

We are walking down a small dirt path in a forest. I suddenly begin to breathe deeply and look around me. I smile as I see the sun shining and the green all around me. There is a donkey with us, pulling an old wooden cart. We are walking behind the cart, and I wonder when we will get in and let the donkey pull us instead of walking.

When I ask him this question, he laughs, and with a smile says, "What do you think, the donkey will do all of the work for you? We will all pull our own weight here". I don't know where we are going, but somehow I'll know when we get there. One thing's for sure, I am free, I am safe, and I am on my own path. I wake up remembering two things: Don't focus on the past, and it's time not to expect others to take me where I need to go. I'm no longer at the mercy of other people's actions because it's my turn to act.

We are all haunted by the ghosts of our past. A ghost can be thought of as a replay of past energy. Like a ripple in a calm lake that pulsates and continues to move through the water in waves, long after the source of the disturbance has passed. Do you remember Newton's law of motion? "An object in motion stays in motion (with the same speed and direction) unless acted upon by an external force." When mass is moving at a certain velocity, we can say that it has momentum. A ghost is a ripple in time. It is a vibration that is still in action or motion due to its momentum. This ghost, however, is still in its direction of motion because it lacks awareness.

Our mental body is filled with ghosts. The ghosts of your past are still moving and acting upon your life. Without awareness, these ghosts continue to haunt your subconscious because their intense emotional sources or feelings are still in momentum. Again, everything is vibration or consciousness, and vibration is felt and not seen. As we will later learn in greater depth, emotion is a vital part of building your reality. Feelings are how we set off, receive, and interpret vibrations or waves of consciousness (thought waves). Awareness is the external force that can change the direction of and transform the vibration. We have the power to shift frequency on the continuum of duality. We are all trapped in a haunted house until we become aware of this and walk out the door never to look back, never to focus our energy in that direction again.

We run on paradigms programmed into us by previous generations, and we continue to move in the direction of these same vibrational patterns. We maintain their habits, experiences, and cycles. Awareness is freedom. It is time to break free from the prison of your past.

All things existing in the physical realm, including inanimate objects, exist on the continuum of duality. Inanimate objects in a home are usually the result of someone's creation. Inanimate objects are made up of the same "vibrational stuff" or consciousness as everything else and are all extensions of the Infinite. Objects, however, are filtered down even more so and therefore lack awareness of their consciousness. This means that inanimate objects are not animated because they lack awareness. They require an outside force or intelligence to co-create and express their potential. They are the Infinite filtered down into a smaller drop of consciousness.

These objects can be bought, made, and obtained with the intention of expression or possession. Food and objects can be shaped by Ego with the intention of possession, grasping, or "holding on". The Guiding Self can also shape objects with the intention of expansion, expression, and nourishment. It is helpful to be aware of this.

Every object contains the seed of both positive and negative since all exist on the same continuum. Either direction can be encouraged and nurtured. When a living creature recalls something from the past, this is called "memory". When an inanimate object holds or retains vibrations (waves of thoughts combined with feelings) of the past, this is called "re-tension". Memory is a recalling of a vibration that has already manifested in physical reality. The difference between memory and retention is "internal recall" versus "external recall". Consciousness and a certain level of awareness give you the power to internally recall vibrations, set them into motion, or give them added momentum. You have the power to do this with any vibration because you are aware of yourself, others, the world, constructs of time, and personal experiences. Awareness brings the power of memory.

Objects lack the awareness of consciousness and hold information or stored vibration in the form of "re-tension". Like a guitar that holds the possibility of music and requires you to pluck a string to produce the combinations of musical notes, objects require an external force, an external interaction to reawaken or stimulate a potential musical note or vibration. They require our awareness to activate their purpose or their potential. As humans, we are in a state of awareness, where we have the power to express and expand our potential. Inanimate objects that lack awareness require OUR awareness to expand and express THEIR potential.

Objects retain information, in the form of vibration, much like a gong that requires you to hit the mallet. The sound that the gong produces varies depending on where and how it is hit. The gong holds the bank of possible vibrations, potential sounds that rely on the mallet, and YOU, to be expressed. We have the power to play objects like musical instruments. If there has been an excess of negative vibrations or feelings around a particular object, they are absorbed and lie dormant until you strike the object with a feeling or emotion that resonates at the same frequency. The object will respond and emit the negative vibrations once again. This is called a haunting. The way to stop a haunting is to become aware of your discord and regain resonance with your Guiding Self. FREE WILL is the power to choose where and how you direct your focus. Focus is a great power, like a laser beam that can create whatever you desire. We control and shape our physical reality, not the other way around.

As we evolve in awareness, we move away from the actions and wants of the Ego, and towards the expression and desires of the soul. We can accomplish this by directing our focus on our feelings, thoughts, actions, and even the food we eat. The vibration put into processed food is a slower vibration that carries the intention of "consuming". These foods do not feed the body or the spirit but instead feed the "Ego-wanting". What is a chocolate cupcake? It is a congealed, physical manifestation of Ego-wanting. All it contains are intentions of "wanting", which in turn make you want more. Processed sugar and other materials are pure Ego-wanting and excite the Ego in all different directions. Use your awareness and your wealth to purchase or eat items that are not from Ego-wanting, but delight the spirit and support you in expressing yourself through all five domains of physical reality.

Let us now look at free radicals in the body to illustrate what it means to "drop to a lower frequency", causing something to vibrate in an "off-balance" way. A free radical is a molecule that is uncharged, which means that it has an unpaired valence electron. Electrons, as you understand them, are subatomic particles that move in orbits around an atom. The valence electrons in the outer orbit find and bond with the electrons of another atom. They come together and contribute one electron each to form a covalent bond. The atoms share and co-create to express and expand their potential.

When a molecule has an unpaired valence electron, it means that one atom does not contribute to the relationship. Instead, it takes away from another out of Ego-wanting. This molecule is now vibrating at a lower frequency and is filled with an insatiable "wanting". This molecule becomes a force of possession and destruction as it seeks out electrons to possess, to fill its void. This void begins to grow in momentum until it becomes cancer. Cancer is the growth of low energy, low electrical charge, or imbalance. There is always an ideal balance or level of sharing in all things. When we are in harmony with this balance, we move towards expansion and expression of potentiality. When we are in discord, acting without awareness, all we create is void.

We must add that we are not saying that you have caused your cancer because your Ego is imbalanced. There are outside forces that come from a place of Ego-wanting. Elements like harmful chemicals, synthetic electromagnetic energy, and other industrial by-products, can affect your system, throw it out of balance, and place cancer into momentum. Sometimes, we do cause cancer as a result of our actions over time, and sometimes others have affected our system. In either case, we use free radicals as a metaphor to explain how "wanting" or "void" differs from desire and expression.

Let us review what we have learned so far before we deepen our understanding. The universe is, at its essence, waves of consciousness that we can describe as vibration. Everything is created from vibration. You have the ability to create from vibration, and you do this whether you are conscious of the process or not. You are a vibrational being who was physically designed by your consciousness to use vibration to create through physical reality. You experience and interpret vibrations as feelings. The creation and expression of your potential in the pursuit of expansion or growth in awareness IS your purpose. You are a fragment of a larger pool of collective consciousness we have called the Guiding Self. There is no need to look externally for spirit guides, angels, or other entities because your Guiding Self is your direct link to the Infinite or the source of all consciousness.

Your desires are your soul's blueprint for evolution. They are instructions from the Creator that teach you and show you how to express your potential. When you express yourself from the vehicle of true desire, you express the Infinite, and your soul or consciousness expands and shines brighter in its radiance. Your desires arise out of coordinates or a certain set of vibrational patterns that your Guiding Self seeks. These desires are fulfilled as you project your essence and radiate more fully into each domain of physical reality.

Central to the Art of Cosmic Creation is the Guiding Star Compass. This is a visual tool that will help you to be aware of what lies beyond the physical. The GSC serves as a reminder that everything is vibration. The GSC reminds you about which specific feelings you desire. These are the coordinates that will help you move in a direction that allows for self-expression and growth of consciousness. The GSC shows you what the Infinite wishes to express through YOU and your purpose that will be carried out through your desires.

Your true desire will be in alignment and harmony with the Guiding Self. Your desire will encourage growth and expansion. It is essential to differentiate between the desires of the Guiding Self and the useless wants of the Ego. The Ego's purpose is to anchor us in physical reality and provide the illusion of being separate so that we may create infinite combinations. The Ego is your tool and not the other way around. The Ego's wants are empty and encourage limitation because this is the Ego's purpose: limiting that which is limitless.

You express the Infinite by expressing your soul. When you create what you desire, everyone else around you and everything around you will have and be more than it was before. It is like a ripple effect throughout existence. You give form to the formless. This is called Cosmic

Creation because we are all stars forming matter out of nothingness, tangible from intangible, something out of nothing. The Art of Cosmic Creation is learning how to consciously engage in the process that is your birthright.

To reach the level of awareness needed to engage with our spirit consciously, we must first become aware of the old paradigms programmed into us. Like a computer, we run on old programs and cycles that are in momentum to keep us trapped and unable to express our true radiance fully. Awareness is the outside force needed to break these cycles. Only then can we fill the conscious mind with programs that move us towards expression on the continuum of duality.

Exercise 2: Rummaging through your Haunted House

Remember all of those boxes in my dream? All of us have these dusty boxes hanging around our subconscious. You don't even know the contents of these long-forgotten containers. Though we can't remember where they came from or why we have them, the truth is, they run our lives by limiting our movement in certain directions and behaviors. Like weeds, they choke our vitality, and our light begins to dim. Imagine you have inherited an old house filled with all of the things that each previous occupant had. Now you are stuck with the culmination of all these things. There is no room for you to put your things away because every spot is taken by things that someone you didn't even know put there.

Now is the time to claim your space. We reclaim our space through vibration. The more you allow your spirit or the Guiding Self to express itself through the domains of physical reality via your coordinates, the more you claim your "space". We are restricted and operate at a lower or limited frequency when our subconscious is cluttered with unnecessary vibrational patterns. We gain the power to walk out and never return by choosing not to focus our energy there again. As a result, we free up energy to focus on desires that will cultivate the vibrations we wrote into our GSC. This act moves the spirit in the direction of expression, expansion, and growth.

Let us now walk into YOUR haunted house so that we can become aware of what lies inside. Once your awareness shifts, the door will open, and you can choose to walk out into freedom or remain in the familiarity of bondage.

As with the previous exercise, take your time. You don't need to fill this out in one sitting. If it helps, look at old photos or talk to siblings, parents, or other family members to help you remember. The time and focus you put into this exercise will be directly proportionate to the awareness you obtain from this exercise. Regardless of what may have been true, concentrate on how things FELT when you go through the questions, and sift through your boxes. Vibration is FELT and not seen. We are looking for the vibrational patterns that are in effect, so it is important to let go of logic and respond based on how you FELT in each category. For example, your parents may have loved you very much, but you FELT unloved because you FELT that they loved a sibling more. Remember, your FEELINGS are the only thing valid here in this exercise. I've included some of my own examples to help guide you.

The Art of Cosmic Creation

Rummaging Through Your Haunted House

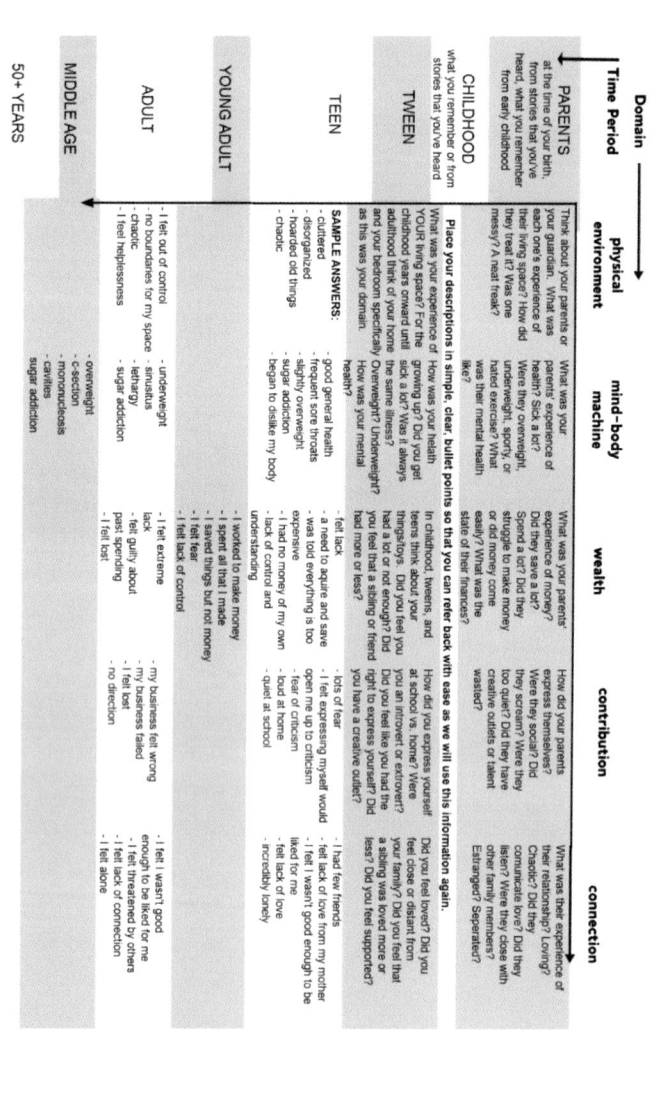

Time Period	physical environment	mind-body machine	wealth	contribution	connection
PARENTS at the time of your birth, from stories that you've heard, what you remember from early childhood	Think about your parents or your guardian. What was each one's experience of their living space? How did they treat it? Was one messy? A neat freak?	What was your parents' experience of health? Sick a lot? Were they overweight, underweight, sporty, or hated exercise? What was their mental health like?	What was your parents' experience of money? Did they save a lot? Spend a lot? Did they struggle to make money or did money come easily? What was the state of their finances?	How did your parents express themselves? Were they social? Did they scream? Were they too quiet? Did they have creative outlets or talent wasted?	What was their experience of their relationship? Loving? Chaotic? Did they communicate love? Did they listen? Were they close with other family members? Estranged? Seperated?
CHILDHOOD what you remember or from stories that you've heard					
TWEEN	Place your descriptions in simple, clear, bullet points so that you can refer back with ease as we will use this information again.				
TEEN	What was your experience of YOUR living space? For the growing up? Did you get childhood years onward until sick a lot? Was it always adulthood think of your home the same illness? and your bedroom specifically Overweight? Underweight? as this was your domain. How was your mental health?		In childhood, tweens, and teens think about your things/toys. Did you feel you had a lot or not enough? Did you feel that a sibling or friend had more or less?	How did you express yourself at school vs. home? Were you an introvert or extrovert? Did you feel like you had the right to express yourself? Did you have a creative outlet?	Did you feel loved? Did you feel close or distant from your family? Did you feel that a sibling was loved more or less? Did you feel supported?
	SAMPLE ANSWERS: - cluttered - disorganized - hoarded old things - chaotic	- good general health - frequent sore throats - slightly overweight - sugar addiction - began to dislike my body	- felt lack - a need to aquire and save - was told everything is too expensive - I had no money of my own - lack of control and understanding	- lots of fear - I felt expressing myself would open me up to criticism - fear of criticism - loud at home - quiet at school	- I had few friends - felt lack of love from my mother - I felt I wasn't good enough to be liked for me - felt lack of love - incredibly lonely
YOUNG ADULT			- I worked to make money - I spent all that I made - I saved things but not money - I felt fear - I felt lack of control		
ADULT	- I felt out of control - no boundaries for my space - chaotic - I feel helplessness	- underweight - sinusitus - lethargy - sugar addiction	- I felt extreme lack - felt guilty about past spending - I felt lost	- my business felt wrong - my business failed - I felt lost - no direction	- I felt I wasn't good enough to be liked for me - I felt threatened by others - I felt lack of connection - I felt alone
MIDDLE AGE		- overweight - c-section - mononucleosis - cavities - sugar addiction			
50+ YEARS					

40

Now take some time to look over the boxes and record your thoughts. Notice how the things your parents did or experienced, have overflowed into your life in one way or another. Become aware of these patterns, and from where they originated. Notice how things have developed as you move through the timeline in each category. None of these things have to be your experience any longer because you have become conscious on another level. You can now see the big picture as you put everything together and understand that you have the ability to create your desire. All of these experiences are the result of unconscious creation. Imagine what you can do now with the gift of awareness?

Let us now clarify the domain of CONTRIBUTION. As we have already described, all five domains of physical reality are vehicles for self-expression. The domain of CONTRIBUTION is how we contribute to the physical world and others around us. This domain begins as the way you communicate yourself to your family and your peers at school. You did this not only through your speech but through creative outlets such as singing, art, sports, etc. This domain is directly linked to your experience in the domain of CONNECTION because it is interpersonal. If you did not feel loved or valued, chances are you stifled your expression out of fear, or changed it to represent a personality that helped you cope with the lack of connection. Lack of Connection stems from feeling unloved or unwanted. This was your protective shield, but like all Ego, this "shield" becomes a cocoon, that will limit and suffocate you, unless you emerge.

The domain of CONTRIBUTION is the way we contribute to the world and show off our best talents and skills. Later on in life, this domain transfers into the arena of career. Become aware of this and notice how you operate in your career. How can your career become a vehicle for Self Expression? How can you find a way to mold and express more of who you are through your career? How can you give to the world in a way that lights up your soul? Walt Disney did this with cartoons. How will you do this? The Guiding Self anchors down into physical reality just as love, and your awareness of connection flows down through all five of your domains.

Notice the order of the five domains. In this exercise, we started with the most physical domain, the Physical Environment. Then, we worked our way upward to the most abstract domain, Connection. We did this because the domains reflect the process of creation, which we will explore later. The order also reflects how the Infinite and the Guiding Self filter down into physical reality. The Guiding self is love, and love is the Guiding Self. Connection experienced as unconditional love filters down through all the domains, and so our experience of love and Connection becomes our experience of everything.

In the next section, we will explore these boxes and become aware of the exact vibrational patterns that we currently run on. This will help you reach new levels of awareness on how to direct your life. We will then revisit the GSC in chapter 4. It is important that you do not skip anything because we are building on each step and creating a momentum of awareness. We're not ready to walk out of the dark yet, but hold on, because we are almost there.

"The Ego gives structure to flow, and destruction makes way for a new beginning"

~Lavender Moon

---

3 LIONS IN THE DARK
HOLDING THE LAMP OF AWARENESS UP TO THE DARKNESS OF IGNORANCE

In a dream...

It's late, and I'm walking home from somewhere. It seems a little darker than usual. The lights of every house are dark, and so I keep to the street where the lamps illuminate the asphalt. I feel as though someone is watching me, and I chalk it up to my imagination.

Suddenly, I hear movement between the trees. A low growl? No, it's only on one side of me, there's a movement to my right and to my left. Something is moving in the dark, and an alarm begins to sound within me. I start running towards my house. I hear something, no, two things chasing me through the street. I'm panicking, and as I reach my door and fumble for the keys, I hear them behind me. I finally get the door open and slam it behind me.

I'm inside, safe. Thankfully, all of the lights are on. I begin to walk up the stairs to my bedroom. Although the lights are on in the stairwell, the lights in the corridor are off, and only darkness stands before me. In the dark, I see two large figures moving. I stop dead in my tracks. Out of the darkness, a large female lion emerges and stands on the steps in front of me.

I feel a female voice speak, I don't hear it, but feel it move through the back of my neck. "Do not be afraid", she says. "Put your hand out". I'm so scared that the lion will pounce on me at any moment, and tear me to shreds. I imagine putting my hand out and the lion grabbing my hand in its jaws. "I can't, it will hurt me", I say frozen in fear. "Do not be afraid, touch her". I reach my hand out, anticipating and bracing myself for the pain of the bite.

My hand reaches her head, and I pet her. I feel my hands move through her soft, warm fur, and she purrs. Her ears go back, and I begin to smile as I scratch between her ears. I feel all of the fear drain from my body, and in its place, a warm exhilaration remains. The second lion, a large male lion, half emerges from the darkness (does he smile at me?) and then moves back into the shadows.

I wake up knowing the dark and fear are only misinterpretations of reality stemming from lack of awareness. Touch your fear, and it becomes your friend.

Fear itself is useful and has a specific purpose. Before we can elaborate on fear, let us reexamine the Ego. The Ego's purpose is to anchor your consciousness in physical reality. The Ego is the device through which the Infinite creates a temporary separation. It is in that perceived separation that we have many minds and imaginations that produce infinite new creations and experiences. The Ego is here to limit us to the physical experience and is therefore concerned with all things physical. Fear is an agent of the Ego, and fear's job is to ensure the survival of your physical vehicle we call the mind-body machine.

Because we are in human form, we possess a unique level of awareness that allows us to live simultaneously in the abstract-symbolic world of "anticipation of possibilities" and imagination, as well as the literal or physical world we experience through the five senses. When we are not aware of who we are, the nature of reality, and the purpose of the Ego, the physical and the abstract become muddled. Fear begins to leak and spillover from its useful physical purpose into all areas of our life.

Fear is a normal physiological response to danger. Fear is a preventative energy, that is necessary, and designed with our survival in mind. What happens when fear has nothing to do with physical danger but instead appears as a result of the Ego directing the imagination? We can define fear as **the anticipation of lack** or the anticipation of having any of the five physical domains taken away from you. Fear is a vibration of helplessness that stems from the misconception that you are "separate" from the Infinite, and this is why fear is an instrument of the Ego. The Ego uses fear to limit you the way a parent might say, "Don't walk into the street or you'll get hit by a car". Fear places parameters around you meant to keep you safe but can be used for manipulation as well.

Fear has its place when your house is on fire or if a lion is actually chasing you, but it holds no purpose beyond the physical. Fear and anxiety are the results of restricting paradigms, or habitual thought patterns still in operation in your subconscious. When you bring these patterns out into the open and expose them to the light of awareness, fear loses its power over you, and you can extend your radiance forward as you engage with and fulfill your desires. As you water fear with unconditional love and acceptance, fear transmutes into strength and power through your ability to radiate. Expression and expansion are impossible if you remain in the vibration of fear. Fear is an instrument of the

Ego. Its only purpose is to limit. Fear is resistance to your desire and the messages of the Guiding Self.

To better understand how to free yourself of fear and its limitations, let us first explain the five levels of awareness. Take a look at the continuum of duality. All things in this universe operate through the continuum of duality. Remember that matter cannot be created nor destroyed, only transformed and so, integration and disintegration work in tandem to create and express the Infinite. When a child is conceived, we can witness the energy of integration and expansion as the DNA of two people come together to create a third being. From there, the cells expand and grow until a baby is created. At the end of one's lifetime, we can witness the power of disintegration. The cells begin to deteriorate until the human dies of old age.

Everything in this physical reality maintains balance in operation through the same continuum. On one end of the spectrum, we have the star shining brightly as it creates and forms all of the building blocks of matter. Imagine that all things on this end of the spectrum are close to the subtle, energetic realms. Remember that stars are a gateway or an entry point from the energetic realm to the physical. Stars are made from the subtle side of physical matter, gases, light, and heat, and so this end of the spectrum vibrates at a very high speed or frequency. The Guiding Self or the non-physical part of you governs this side of the continuum. The Guiding Self is the part of you that is a vast pool of collective consciousness filtered down from the Infinite. You express the Infinite, and you reflect the Infinite.

On the other end of the spectrum, we find the heavenly body known as *the black hole*. A black hole occurs when there is a mass so dense, so compact, and so heavy, moving at such a slow rate of vibration that it pulls everything down with it, including light rays. At this end of the spectrum, everything vibrates at such a slow rate or a low frequency that it limits, catches, possesses, consumes, and sucks everything into a perpetual state of immobility. This is the realm of the Ego where possession dominates over expression. This is where the "want" of the Ego dominates over "desire" of the Guiding Self.

The Continuum of Duality

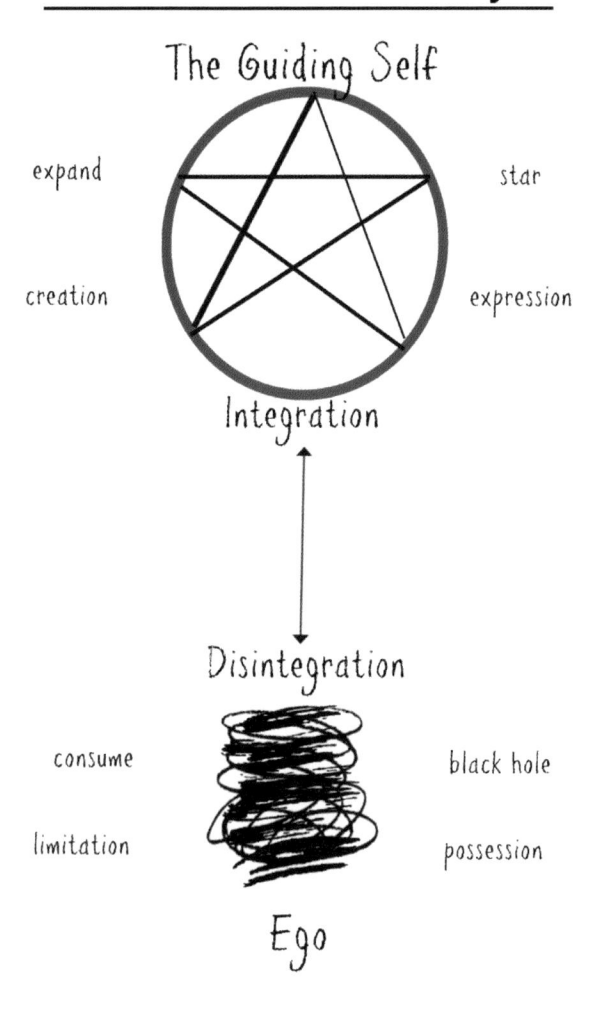

The Guiding Self

expand

star

creation

expression

Integration

↕

Disintegration

consume

black hole

limitation

possession

Ego

As we have already explained, Ego is not bad. The Ego and the black hole have a purpose. They are here to anchor and limit that which cannot be harnessed or limited. The Ego is a temporary structure used for separation so that we may create infinite possibilities and experiences. This universe requires both energies to remain in operation. The Ego gives structure to flow, and destruction makes way for a new beginning. To become a Cosmic Creator, we must understand how to work with the continuum instead of allowing it to work you. You do this through the light of awareness.

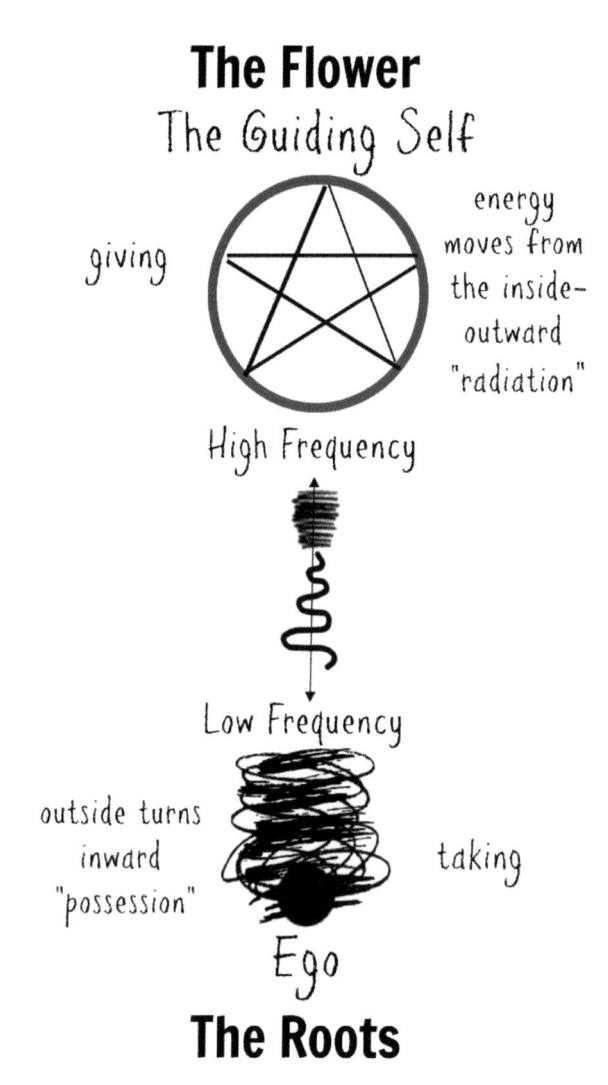

The Flower
The Guiding Self

giving

energy moves from the inside-outward "radiation"

High Frequency

Low Frequency

outside turns inward "possession"

taking

Ego

The Roots

A special note about fear:
Fear moves you towards the Ego and away from the Guiding Self, your true identity or spirit. As you move towards the energy of the "black hole", your vibration lowers, energy turns inward and you move away from self-expression and growth. You find yourself in a state of arrested development and mental slavery. It is ignorance that enslaves you as it conceals light.

There are five levels of awareness that allow our consciousness to move upward on the continuum until we are aligned with the Guiding Self. The first level, located at the bottom of the continuum, is called the **Level of Entry**. Let us use the development of a human to explain each level of awareness. Imagine a fetus before it is born. The unborn child exists through the **Level of Entry**. Here, the unborn child has consciousness and a basic awareness but lacks knowledge of the self. Right now, the fetus is a series of electrical impulses and automatic functions. It lives and grows in the womb's darkness, completely dependent upon its surroundings, its mother. The unborn child has no independent thought or desire beyond those related to survival; it just exists.

The next level of awareness is the **Level of Self**. This is where we become aware of the "**me**" and the **"I"**. You can see this clearly in the small child. The baby or young child can only recognize their base wants or needs and cannot yet see or understand others' points of view besides **I**, **me**, and **mine**. It is important to note that there is no awareness of the Infinite, there is only the self as it should be at this point, to be anchored in physical reality. After this, there is the **Level of Other**. This is where we become aware of others as we grow to see and feel their perspectives. We can see this level of awareness emerge in teens as they become increasingly concerned with their peers' opinions and views.

The third level is where most humans reside. For most of us, our level of awareness will end here, and we will move through life on autopilot. We operate on the preconditioned thought patterns and habits of our parents, teachers, and larger society or religion. While operating on someone else's program, we always have that nagging feeling that something is missing and that we are unfulfilled. Some ignore this and move on in their lives like robots acting from old programming, and others fill the void with addictions. When you fill the void with more void, your vibration rate drops so much that you create your own black hole that consumes everything in its path, including your light.

The fourth level of awareness is the **Level of Awakening**. This is where a part of you awakens as you realize that you are more than your body and mind. At this point, you begin to understand how the body and mind work together. You become aware that up until now, you have been running on old programs that do not serve you. You then understand how the mind operates like a computer, and that the body carries out the mind's commands. You know that this is how you have shaped your reality up until now and understand how to change your reality where you are not satisfied.

The fifth level is the awareness of the Infinite and The Guiding Self. This is the **Level of Cosmic Creation**, where you understand that all is vibration and that you have the power to mold vibration because you reflect and express the Infinite through carrying out your desire. People become afraid or anxious when they focus on lack or what they don't have instead of a desire to create something new. This person forgets they are an extension of the Infinite and therefore become unaware of their creative potential.

The Five Levels of Awareness

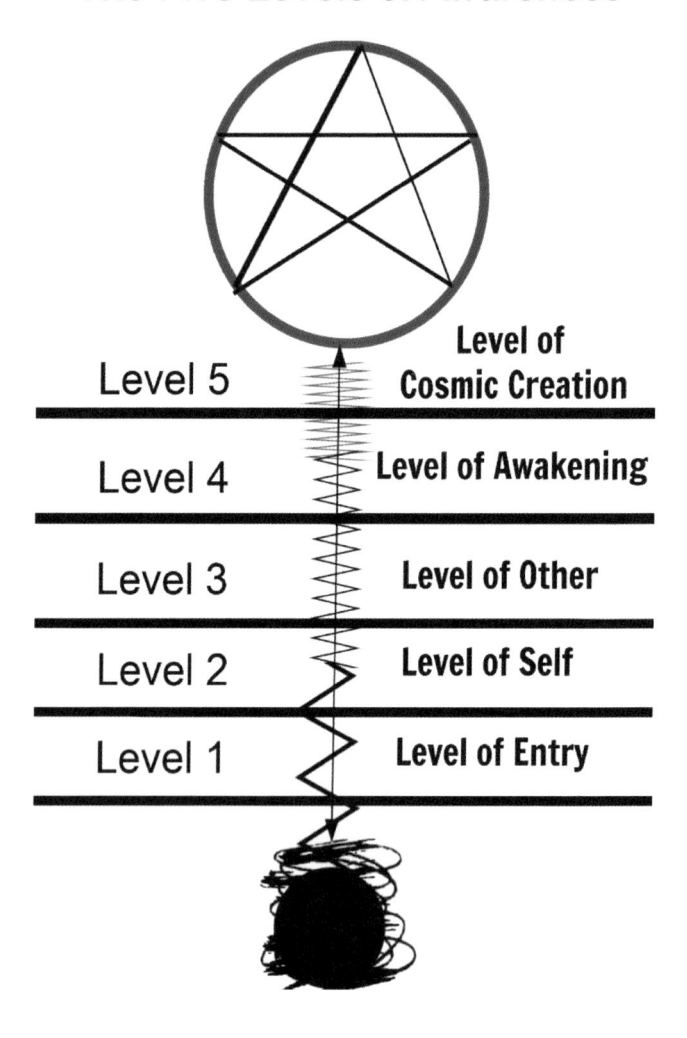

Level 5	Level of Cosmic Creation
Level 4	Level of Awakening
Level 3	Level of Other
Level 2	Level of Self
Level 1	Level of Entry

As we develop our higher awareness, we transcend the perceived limits set forth by the Ego. As we connect with the Guiding Self, we bring our greatest passions into physical reality. A Cosmic Creator looks at everything through the lens of the Guiding Self and not the Ego. Cosmic Creators are aware of their limitless potential and, therefore, do not need to engage in the lower vibrations of fear and doubt. Remember that one side of the continuum anchors you into physical reality, and the other side connects you with the Infinite. You express and reflect the Infinite through the **five domains of physical reality**. Everything you create has an energetic counterpart on the same continuum, so you vibrationally expand and create energetically as you do so physically.

Fear comes from the misconception that you are separate from the Infinite. Fear is an instrument of the Ego. Fear's purpose is to limit and contain you. Fear is useful for preserving the physical body when it is in physical danger, but beyond this, it has no use. Fear moves awareness towards the Ego and away from The Guiding self, your true identity, or spirit. As you move towards the energy of the black hole, your vision lowers, energy turns inward, and you move away from self-expression and growth. You find yourself in a state of arrested development and mental slavery. It is ignorance that enslaves you as it conceals the light of awareness. Let us now move into the **Level of Awakening** as we begin to understand how the conscious and subconscious mind work together.

The mind can be thought of as the computer that runs the body. This is why we refer to the physical vehicle, as the **mind-body machine**, because it is just that. Cosmic Creators understand that they are pure intelligence streaming into the **mind-body machine**, much like virtual reality or the movie Avatar. When we become aware of who we are, we begin to understand how to operate this **mind-body machine** to express our essence through our creations in physical reality. To do this, we must understand the laws of operation that allow you to direct and control the mind-body machine.

The moving parts to the equation reflect the levels of awareness that we have discussed. In this section, you will learn how the Infinite, Guiding Self, conscious mind, subconscious mind, and body all work together, and are all necessary ingredients for Cosmic Creation. When one part is disconnected, the "circuit will not light", and you will not be able to manifest your desire. When all are working together and in open communication with one another, your desire will condense itself into physical reality.

The Guiding Self:

The Guiding Self mediates between the Infinite and the partial self. The Guiding Self holds a seed containing the exact code or coordinates or instructions that contain your soul's blueprint for evolution. When you are born into a physical reality, it requires you to "fall" (or a piece of you anyway), because your consciousness becomes temporarily fused with the Ego to be anchored into physical reality. This fusion produces the **partial self**, the part of you that is anchored into physical reality. After this, it is your purpose and birthright to ascend, to stand upright once again towards the light of awareness in physical form. Desire is the vehicle through which you ascend. Desire is your unique set of instructions for ascension. This is what needs to be taught to children. Teach this to your children so that the world may expand in consciousness at a faster rate.

The Conscious Mind:

The conscious mind mediates between the Guiding Self and the subconscious mind. [In reality, nothing is linear, but we describe everything in the dimensions that best suit the human brain. We use concepts that are more digestible for the human psyche.] The conscious mind links with subtle vibrations or waves of consciousness and interacts with the subconscious mind and its programming. The subconscious establishes those vibrations into physical form or neural pathways. The conscious mind receives messages from the Guiding Self in the form of vibration or frequency and translates or converts those frequencies, and shapes them into pictures, images, and ideas. This is where co-creation occurs, and the part of you that is temporarily separate, (the partial self), receives communication from the Infinite. It is here that awareness is crucial because if we are not aware of where and how our ideas come to us, we mistake them as useless and meaningless, or we even fear them through the darkness of our ignorance. When we understand these images and ideas as communication from the Guiding Self, we become open to receiving them, and in turn, the guidance begins to flow regularly.

In other words, the conscious mind has two main functions. One is to receive impressions from the Guiding Self, and the other is to focus attention. The more you are consciously aware of yourself as an extension of the Infinite, the greater your ability to focus. The Infinite gives us "Free Will", or the ability to choose a focus. This will be explained in greater depth in Chapter 5.

The Subconscious Mind:
The subconscious mind mediates between the conscious mind and the physical body. This is the part of our mind that interfaces with the physical and engraves

subtle vibration in the form of thought waves into the physical flesh as neural pathways. The subconscious can be seen as a coder, scribe, or sculptor that takes in the information or stimuli from the brain and interprets or translates them into feelings. These feelings further filter down into emotions. When the feelings interface with the existing program or paradigms of the subconscious, they produce emotions. Emotions can be interpreted as vibrations or waves of consciousness that are lower in frequency, so they can enter into the cytoplasm of each cell and cause them to vibrate at a specific rate. Cells begin to "carve-out" or "etch" or "engrave" neural pathways to establish neural-circuitry that link up emotions to physical sensations. Hormones are secreted, and patterns are established. The result is that the body begins to take on specific actions and develop certain habits that in turn, shape the five domains of your life.

Repeated emotions solidify as neural-pathways or physical channels in the body that create automatic responses, patterns, and habits. In short, you can say that your subconscious controls how you act and think, and this, in turn, creates your reality. The subtle becomes physical through a series of "defining, slowing down, shaping, and engraving". When the programs or networks established in the subconscious are not in harmony with the Guiding Self, you cannot manifest your desires into physical reality. It is like we come with a startup program established by the Ego that ensures survival until our brains and levels of awareness are developed to a certain degree. Until then, we remain on autopilot as a safety precaution.

The Ego uses fear and doubt to shape pathways that limit risk. The pathways of connection and faith have not yet been established to the same degree, or were not etched or engraved into the **mind-body machine**. The code can only be re-programmed or re-written as a result of higher states of awareness. This is where we can make a difference and program according to our Guiding Star Compass. When the Guiding Self and the subconscious mind are in alignment, we become conscious Cosmic Creators. We control the focus of our minds and the actions or habits of our bodies that shape and mold the **five domains of physical reality**.

The Body:

The body mediates between the subconscious mind and the physical world around us, or the **five domains of physical reality**. As the subconscious mind and body interface, the subtle is converted into physical. Emotions are converted into actions and habits, which create physical results. Are you currently manifesting from your limited Ego or your limitless spirit? Before we can accomplish all of this, we must first become aware of what the Ego has programmed into us, so that we may reverse it, rework, or rewire the circuitry. Let us bring the codes that no longer serve us, that create unneeded anxiety and fear in our lives into the light so that we may "touch them", and turn our fear into a friend or guide. Remember that everything carries the seed of positive or negative because all exist on the same continuum and only vary by degree. In the next chapter, we will go deeper into transforming these negative fears into positive programs.

Exercise 3: Holding the Lamp of Awareness up to your Lions in the Dark

In the last exercise, we began to uncover the patterns and habits that we run on. We are now aware that these patterns are not our own and that the program that is in current operation does not support the desire of the Guiding

Self. You are now beginning to understand that at first, we build our life around a wound. Only the Ego can be wounded. Because of its nature, it is meant to limit and to separate. It is a misconception of "separateness" that causes the wound. When we hold the lamp of awareness up to the limiting program, we become consciously aware of the code and can rewrite the code to our desire.

Fear disintegrates in the presence of the Guiding Self. Let us now uncover the specific programs that have been running your life and creating your current domains of physical reality. As with the previous exercise, find a quiet place where you are undisturbed. Take out your Haunted House exercise. Look over the boxes for the time period of **Parents** and look through the patterns of each domain.

Step 1: Focus on the domain of **Physical Environment**. Look over the patterns in your box and ask yourself:

What message did these behaviors or experiences send to me about my physical environment?

What did these patterns teach me? What were these patterns saying to me about how I experienced this domain?

For example:

My box for **Parents** in the domain of **Physical Environment**:

-Dad was sloppy, messy and saved everything.
-Mom was always cleaning and throwing things out.

Step 2: I examine those two patterns and notice how they do not agree with each other. They don't complement one another. They are in conflict, and conflict stresses me out.

Step 3: I look for the negative message these patterns sent to me or imprinted within my psyche. I conclude that "my physical environment is filled with tension and stress".

Step 4: Place this core message into your new **Lamp of Awareness table** in the corresponding time period and domain.

Repeat this exercise one time period at a time, and only one domain at a time so that your next box will be [Parents - **Mind-Body Machine**], and then [Parents - **Wealth**], and so on, working your way horizontally.

The Lamp of Awareness

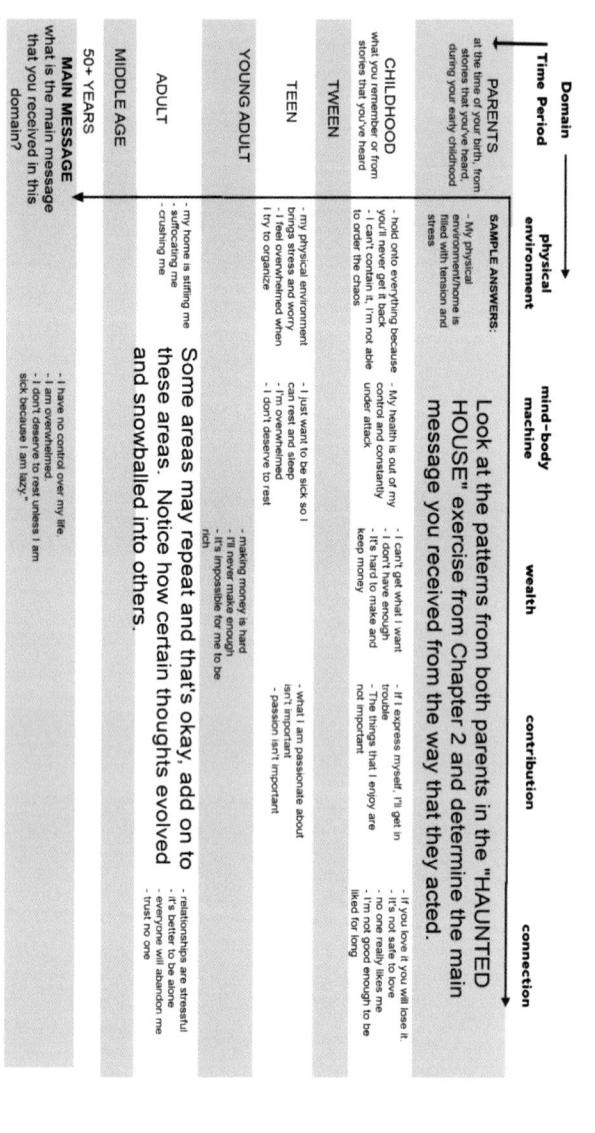

Domain →

Time Period	physical environment	mind-body machine	wealth	contribution	connection
PARENTS — at the time of your birth, from stories that you've heard, during your early childhood	**SAMPLE ANSWERS:** - My physical environment/home is filled with tension and stress				
CHILDHOOD — what you remember or from stories that you've heard	- hold onto everything because you'll never get it back - I can't contain it, I'm not able to order the chaos	- My health is out of my control and constantly under attack	- I can't get what I want - I don't have enough - It's hard to make and keep money	- If I express myself, I'll get in trouble - The things that I enjoy are not important	- If you love it you will lose it - It's not safe to love - no one really likes me - I'm not good enough to be liked for long
TWEEN	- my physical environment brings stress and worry - I feel overwhelmed when I try to organize	- I just want to be sick so I can rest and sleep - I'm overwhelmed - I don't deserve to rest		- what I am passionate about isn't important - passion isn't important	
TEEN					
YOUNG ADULT	- my home is stifling me - suffocating me - crushing me		- making money is hard - I'll never make enough - It's impossible for me to be rich		- relationships are stressful - it's better to be alone - everyone will abandon me - trust no one
ADULT					
MIDDLE AGE					
50+ YEARS					
MAIN MESSAGE — what is the main message that you received in this domain?	- I have no control over my life - I am overwhelmed - I don't deserve to rest unless I am sick because I am lazy				

Look at the patterns from both parents in the "HAUNTED HOUSE" exercise from Chapter 2 and determine the main message you received from the way that they acted.

Some areas may repeat and that's okay, add on to these areas. Notice how certain thoughts evolved and snowballed into others.

Let's try one more example:

By the time you reach your teens, your program is already established, but it continues to grow in momentum like a snowball and defines itself. Let's see what this looks like...

Step 1: Look at my box for the time period of **Middle Age** and the domain of **Mind-Body Machine**. Here are the patterns/ experiences for that box:

- C-section
- Overweight
- Epstein-Barr
- Cavities
- Chronic sore throats
- Sinusitis

Step 2: I examine these patterns, and not only examine what was happening, but how I felt as they were happening, and I realized that during this time period, I spent a great deal of time feeling overwhelmed and exhausted.

Step 3: I saw the message or the belief that I was using these circumstances to reinforce: "My health is under constant attack. My health is out of my control. I just want to be sick, so I can rest. I feel overwhelmed."

When you have completed your chart, look through each domain vertically, and contemplate the development and definition of paradigms and subconscious programming within each domain. Start with the domain of *Physical Environment* and at the time of *"Parents"*. Read on vertically until you reach your current time period. Notice the main message that pervades each time period. What is the main limiting or negative message that has developed within each domain? Write this main message for each domain in the final row marked "Main Message".

For example, as I looked through my domain of *Mind-Body Machine*, I realized that I used illness as a way to cope with overwhelm and chaos. The main message or paradigm that I was running on was, "I have no control over my life. I am overwhelmed. I don't deserve to rest unless I am sick because I am lazy."

As you are beginning to understand, each of these limiting programs stem from the misunderstanding that you are *less than*; that you are imperfect and undeserving of unconditional love and acceptance. This, in turn, comes from the lack of awareness that you express and reflect the Infinite, and that you exist on the same continuum as the Infinite, and in a way, you are one in the same, only varying by degree.

It is out of this darkness of ignorance that all of your fears are born. As we bring these hidden programs out into the light of awareness, we can understand how and why they developed. Through the lens of the Guiding Self, we can look back on these limiting paradigms with unconditional love and understand that these beliefs are the soil and the fertilizer that we have chosen before birth, to grow the garden that we desire. Remember that negative holds the seed of positive and vice versa.

"Fear comes from the misconception that you are separate from the Infinite"

~Lavender Moon

---

4 COLUMBIA
WHO'S DRIVING YOU?

In a dream…

Oh wow, he's actually calling me? I can't believe he wants to meet me! Wait a minute, it's after 11:00 PM, and I don't feel right about going out this late. Why does he want to meet me now? Oh, what the heck, he wants to meet me! I'm so lucky. I quickly tell him on the phone that I'll be ready and looking for his car outside. I throw all of my concerns away in exchange for his attention.

It's midnight when he arrives in the yellow cab, driven by a friend I have never seen before. Disappointment soon floods my awareness as he tells me to get into the cab's back seat, but I don't complain, for fear that he won't want to hang out with me. I get in and sit alone in the backseat. I feel sad, dejected, not in alignment with myself, and helpless, as he and his friend continue to talk, never once acknowledging me or including me in their conversation.

"He will talk to me when we get there," I tell myself with a forced smile. But where are we going and what are we doing? I remain quiet in exchange for being given the privilege of being in his presence. I continue to feel uneasy as we drive on, getting deep into upper Manhattan, around

Columbia University. He and his friend begin to argue, and this argument becomes heated. I'm a passive, silent witness to all of this. I keep up the hope that he might turn around and notice me, but it never happens.

Suddenly, they both stop the car and yell at me to get out. It's around 2:00 AM by now, and I'm frightfully aware that I'm at least two hours away from my home, and have only enough money for a subway ride. "You can't just leave me here! I want to go home!" They scream at me again to get out, and I do, and there I am in an unsafe place at 2:00 AM, all by myself, and my only ticket back home on the subway is an even less safe alternative. I traded in my safety, happiness, power, and possibly my life for the promise of attention.

I feel a mixture of fear, shame, anger, sadness, and frustration. I regain my senses and look around me. I recognize the area; I'm in front of the dorms of Columbia University. I see a group of students walking in a little drunk, and I quickly get into the middle of their group as they flash their ID's to the security guard. Tired himself, the security guard just lazily waves us inside.

Once I get inside, I walk upstairs to the dorms. I feel better now that I am inside, but my intense fear for my safety gives way to extreme anxiety that I might get caught without a school ID, and possibly arrested for trespassing. I figure that if I can stay out of the hallway, I'll be safer. I quickly enter the girl's bathroom as another student exits, since I don't have the key. I wash my face and wonder what to do. I walk out and lie down on the couch in the hallway. Students are always studying, and it wouldn't be weird if I were to sleep here, only I don't have any books with me. What if someone tells me to go to my room? The anxiety is almost too much to take.

I walk down the hallway and find a storage room. It has cleaning supplies, and I figure it isn't likely to be used in the middle of the night. Bingo! I make myself space and sit down in the darkness, ever vigilant and alert to every possible noise and possible danger that could happen. Then, somehow, I doze off, and when I wake up. I look at my watch, and it's 6:30 AM. I made it, and it's morning.

I feel the anxiety drain away and in its place, pure joy. I skip out the front door. "Have a great day!" I say to the security guard. I walk out and breathe in the fresh morning air. I walk down the street, and suddenly I am turning the corner to my house. I notice that my shoes are off, and I focus on the feeling of my bare feet, contently walking on the warm concrete. "I am so happy, I am home," I say to myself, "I'm safe." It's hard to describe, but I feel stable and grounded, standing on my own two feet, carrying me in the direction that I desire.

As I wake up, I laugh and say aloud, "I'll never let anyone drive me again!" Like my dream, you are in the car because of someone else's instructions, being driven by someone else, whom you have never met before...

As we have already learned, we are on autopilot, but it's nothing to feel bad about or beat yourself up over. You are a magnificent being, a droplet of the Infinite. You have chosen to descend into physical reality to experience different states of consciousness and create from these many states. To do this, you had to anchor yourself into a seemingly "separate" body with a seemingly "separate" personality. You had to forget your true, divine nature, to be a "separate" being. However, if you are reading these words at this very moment, you are now ready to remember who you are, and who you are is Infinite.

Before you can become a Cosmic Creator, we must first consciously rework the programming we discovered in the last chapter. Together, we will rework your neural-circuitry that was carved out by the subconscious mind. We will install a new program that will support your spirit's expression through all five domains of reality, in the attainment of your desire. Together we will release you from the limitations placed upon you by family, society, and culture, so that you are free to finally come home to your true authentic self.

Understand that we are projectors. We are quite literally projecting our internal script outward onto physical reality. Remember that imagination is the **projective** part of intuition. The entire universe is, in fact, consciousness. We create the physical reality around us through our thoughts, beliefs, and imagination. Imagination and the things we imagine radiate outward into the five domains of physical reality, shaping our everyday experiences. We begin to attract what we think and feel the most. Every molecule and atom begins to arrange itself around us according to our internal thoughts and projections.

As you become aware of your creative power, notice what your dominant thoughts and feelings are. What do you imagine and think about the most? Become aware of how the beliefs we uncovered in Chapter 3, still echo throughout your daily life. Notice how these thoughts play out in each of your five domains. If you take each coordinate and write down the opposite feeling, you will notice the predominant feelings that you have experienced throughout your current life. These feelings are the vibrating results of limiting programs. In the following example, we can begin to understand how everything holds the seed of the opposite.

For example:

GSC Coordinate	Opposite Feeling
I feel free	I feel trapped
I feel beautiful	I feel ugly
I feel powerful	I feel weak/helpless
I feel open	I feel closed off
I feel connected	I feel alone

Changing your programming and internal dialogue starts with the awareness that we are creative beings and have full dominion over our physical experience. Look back on your life and notice how much you've created unconsciously. Now imagine how much you can create by consciously directing your mental energy. You have the power to choose your internal script and what you will project outward onto your five domains of physical reality.

Notice for one day, without judgment, which thoughts and feelings predominately rule your day. Notice your internal and external speech, and you will realize that your internal thoughts and programs are playing out in your everyday life. Do you argue with another in your mind? You will find arguments in physical reality. Are you telling yourself and coworkers that you're under-appreciated at work? If so, you will find yourself being underappreciated in physical reality.

We will now speak to you about the difference between reaching from the Ego versus radiating from the Guiding Self. When you are unaware of your true identity and begin to misidentify your consciousness with the anchor that is the Ego, you become finite and limited in your thoughts. If you're finite and limited, you are limited in what you can be, do, have, or possess. Those are the thoughts that the Ego is concerned with, 'possession, and power over'. Remember that the Ego's job is to limit us by anchoring our consciousness into the mind-body machine. Our job is simply to be aware that the Ego is a mechanism necessary to operate a mind-body machine, but it is not our essence. When we mistakenly see the world through the Ego's eyes, everything becomes a struggle to possess, contain, and control something that, in reality, is Infinite.

This struggle to control is a misconception of the Ego. The Ego, fear of lack, and perceived loss of power and control, begins to create something akin to fear, known as anxiety. Remember that we define fear as *the anticipation of loss in one or all of the five domains*. Anxiety is *the perceived lack of power or control over one or all of your five domains*. The Ego uses anxiety to focus your thoughts around people and circumstances out of your direct control. We call this obsessive focusing, **mental grasping**. We participate in mental grasping when we obsessively focus our thoughts on exerting control over another's actions, the weather, traffic, negativity of the past, future, or anything else that takes us in the opposite direction of our desires. Mental grasping is reaching from your Ego, and all this does is dim your light or bury your essence deeper inside the mud, instead of helping it grow upward and outward into the light of day.

When we let go of the illusion of control and release our mental grasping, we can begin to embrace our true essence. We define real power as your ability to expand and radiate like a star, projecting your light outward, onto physical reality. We order our world by expanding from our Source. We do not accomplish anything by trying to exert external control over people, events, or circumstances. There is no control, only creation. Your creations hold consciousness. Everything grows and expands. Your Guiding Star Compass helps you to be aware of the direction in which you are moving. When something you have begun to grow takes shape, focus the mind on projecting outward, and release your mental grasping. Let go of the illusion of control and continue to observe and wonder at your creations just as you would observe and become surprised by the actions and words of a growing child.

To understand how we form our physical reality on a deeper level, let us speak again about stars and action versus attraction. A star maintains its form through two "directions" or forces. These forces are the outward push of fusion and the inward pull of gravity. As long as the star retains its form, it can continue to give birth to new elements, which will continue to take shape. Our creations are brought into physical form by the same two forces: The outward projective force of action, and the inward, magnetic pull of attraction. All forms of creation in physical reality are a product of these two forces or directions. The atom itself maintains its form from the outward push of electricity and the inward pull of electromagnetic energy.

The actions we take inform the ether and subsequently what we attract into our lives: **action + attraction = physical manifestation**. Actions include thoughts, feelings, speech, and habits. Actions are what we project towards something or someone. Based on these projections, we begin to shape our reality. These actions will take us in one of two directions; towards our desire and help us form that desire, or they will take us away from our desire and cause it to disintegrate. This is why many of us have goals that never seem to take shape and coalesce into physical reality.

Thoughts infused with feelings are actions, and it is these actions that attract and shape your reality. When we run on the programs of our past or the programs of conditioning from our family, culture, or society, it becomes THEY who are creating our reality. It is like being taken far away from home and being dropped in a strange location that brings us anxiety and fear. These feelings are useful information because they let us know that we are moving in the wrong direction, away from the Guiding Self.

The *Law of Inertia* states that an object in motion stays in motion unless acted upon by an outside force. We can rewrite this law as: "A wave of consciousness (thought infused with feeling) stays in momentum unless awareness and the opposite thought waves are applied". We have already become aware of the projections we are using to maintain the form of our current reality. Now, we will apply the second part of this formula to rewrite the script of these programs.

Exercise 4: Coming Home

Step 1: List your "Main Messages" from your "Lamp of Awareness" chart in chapter 3, into the "Coming Home" chart under "Main Limiting Messages". Notice that we have changed the order of the domains and we will explain why later.

Step 2: Examine each thought, one at a time. Start with the main message from the domain of "Connection". As you read the limiting message, breathe and let go of any judgment by saying to yourself that this belief belongs to someone else and how wonderful and exciting it is to be able to choose a new one. Then ask your Guiding Self: How can I move this program upward on the Continuum of Duality? How can I change this message into a positive message that encourages my self-expression and growth?

For example, "I'm not good enough to love" can become, "I am a unique expression of the Infinite, perfect in every way. Unconditional love constantly flows to me and through me".

Within each positive message, place a "feeling word"
I feel_____.

For example, "I feel joy and freedom as I freely give and receive unconditional love".

Step 3: Now, state each empowering message and try to feel that new feeling in your heart as you say this message to yourself. Place your attention, consciousness, or awareness, on the center of your chest and notice any physical sensations that come up there.

Coming Home
Discovering your Treatments

Domain	Limiting Message	Empowering Message
Connection	**SAMPLE ANSWER:** it's not safe to love or to be loved.	I feel joy and freedom as I give and receive unconditional love.
Contribution		
Wealth	The limiting messages become your "treatments" or your specific messages that your subconscious requires to reach your goals.	
Mind-Body Machine	I can only rest when I am sick.	I rest and relax in radiant health.
Physical Environment	The darkness holds the seeds of light, the negative contains the positive and vice versa	

Remember that your life experiences are the soil that you chose to grow in; your past holds the seeds to the future.

The Guiding Star Compass

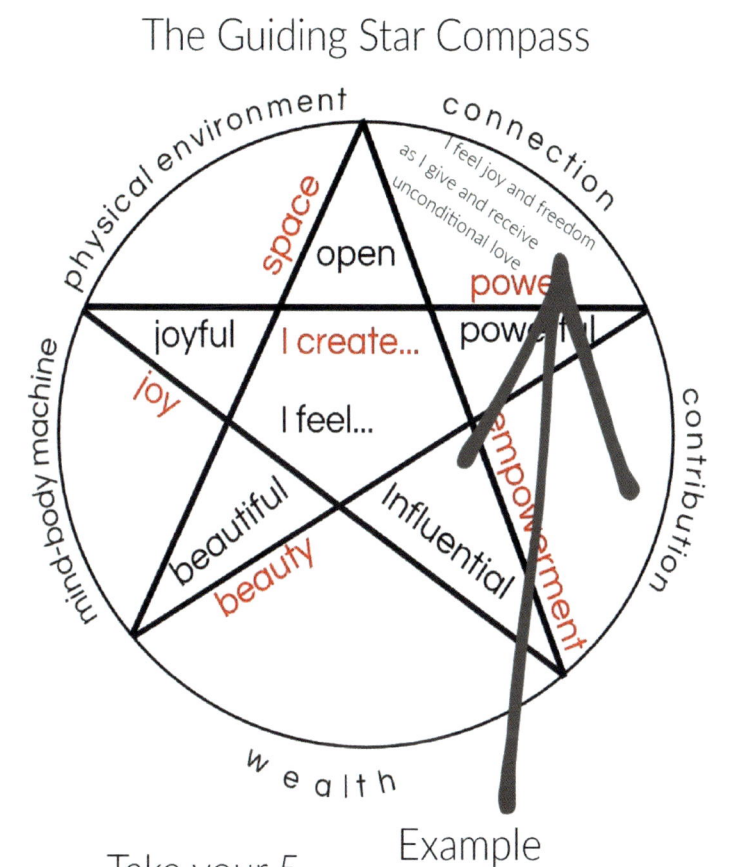

Take your 5 treatments and place them into your Guiding Star Compass

Example treatment for the domain of connection: I feel joy and freedom as I give and receive unconditional love.

My Guiding Star Compass

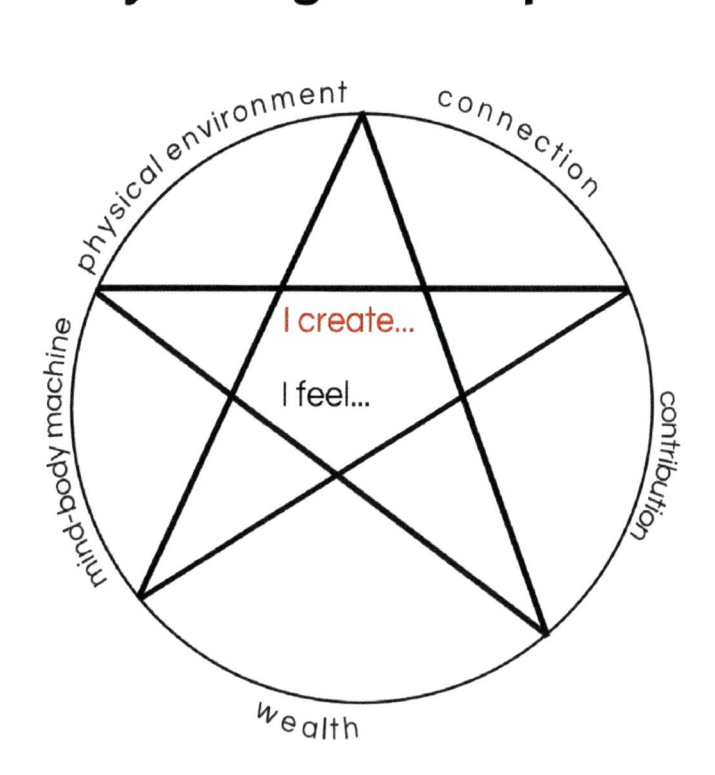

- physical environment
- connection
- contribution
- wealth
- mind-body machine

I create...

I feel...

> "The actions we take inform the ether and subsequently what we attract into our lives"
>
> ~Lavender Moon

5 THE PARTY
THE POWER TO CHOOSE YOUR REALITY

In a dream...

I'm at a party in a big house. Lots of people are here, and this one, very drunk guy keeps trying to hit on me. I tell him politely that I'm not interested, but he doesn't seem to listen.

I finally say in a loud voice, "I SAID I'M NOT INTERESTED!" He turns to walk away and spills his coffee all over my white shirt, laughs, and says, "Oops, sorry, ha, ha, ha."

I'm outraged that this jerk has ruined my shirt. All I can feel is anger and frustration. I walk over to an old man, (the same one from the haunted house, as it turns out). He is sitting in the middle of the living room. I turn to him and say, "Did you see what that guy just did to me? Can you believe that jerk? He ruined my shirt. He just ruined it!"

But the old man doesn't seem to be paying attention to me. Instead, he stares ahead at something with a peaceful gaze. He suddenly turns his face towards me, rolls his eyes at me, and turns back to whatever he was looking at.

I become even more infuriated that on top of the other jerk, THIS jerk rolled his eyes at me and didn't agree with me about the OTHER jerk. I suddenly say, "Are you even listening to me? What is your problem? What are you even looking at?"

As I am speaking, I turn my head in the direction of his gaze and see the most beautiful green, glowing, mango tree growing right in the center of the living room.

The tree is glowing with a bright halo and has green mangoes hanging from the branches that sparkle like emeralds. As my eyes adjust to the light emanating from the tree, I realize these are not mangoes but prismatic beings that almost look like praying mantises hanging upside down, like embryos. I am in awe of the majesty of this sight, and slowly sit down next to the old man, speechless.

In some wordless way, I understand what this tree is. It's the entire universe; we are all connected through the branches by one root. None of us are separate and the beings are each of us, the fruit of the Infinite; developing, expanding, and ripening with awareness at a perfect rate. I feel completely amazed as I say out loud, "I didn't even see it because I was looking down at my shirt the whole time" And then as a new awareness enters my being, I start to laugh. "It's only an old t-shirt, not even my favorite, I'll just put it in the washing machine" And I just sit there, wordless, next to the old man, taking in this magical tree.

I wake up and understand that this tree is a symbol of life. I realize that in every moment, I have a choice. I can keep on staring at my dirty shirt and focus on what is wrong or missing from my life, or I can look at my life and everything in it as a gift, the fruit of my own creation. You have this power, too, and you have the power to choose your reality in every moment.

In the last chapter, you may have noticed that we changed the order of our domains. Why do we start with the domain of *Connection*? Why did we change the direction of our domains in the last exercise? The Infinite and the Guiding Self vibrate at the frequency of unconditional love. This is pure love, not based on your actions or successes, but on the fact that you EXIST. You are an integral part of everything in this universe. Without you, all consciousness could never move forward and the world as we know it could never exist.

The reason why we don't have what we desire in life or feel like something indescribable is missing, is because when we descend into physical reality, we have to forget who we are in order to create INFINITE possibilities. In our descent, we are anchored by the Ego into the individual "me", and when we are born, our families and society begin to create and shape our Ego's identity.

We begin to learn that we are separate and at the mercy of luck and circumstance. We learn that we have to earn love and that love can easily be taken away when we do or say something that is considered "wrong". We misinterpret love as approval and forget that we are an unconditionally loved spark of the Infinite. It is this disconnection from unconditional love that separates us from the Guiding Self and wisdom of the Infinite. We no longer vibrate at a frequency where we can hear the Guiding Self.

Like a bat who has lost her ability to echolocate, we indeed find ourselves in the darkness with no "north star" to guide us home. We find ourselves at the mercy of our external circumstances. Reconnecting to unconditional love is the first step towards communication with the Guiding Self. We define unconditional love as the point of contact or connection between the partial self and the Guiding Self, between the Guiding Self and the Infinite. Understand that you are unconditionally loved because you exist. Be aware that you are connected to everything, to all of life, and understand that you are never alone.

Just as love is the frequency and the language through which the Guiding Self communicates, fear is the frequency and the language of the Ego. The Ego's purpose is to limit you so as to keep you anchored in physical reality. The Ego's stronghold is in the body, and it's lower energy centers. The Ego is what keeps your consciousness fused to this physical vessel (the mind-body machine), but be aware that it is not you. The frequency of fear focuses you on "lack" or "the anticipation of having any of the five domains taken away from you or injured". If you remain in the frequency of fear by running on your past programs, you will live and operate in limitation, through seeking to possess out of the fear of loss. You will attract loss.

By learning to speak the language of unconditional love, you will begin to hear your Guiding Self very clearly. This is the force of attraction we are talking about. The Guiding Self will be your shining star in the darkness, continually guiding you towards your desire. As you take the actions of unconditional love by thinking and feeling these new thoughts, you will begin to resonate at the frequency of unconditional love, bringing expression and expansion into your life. Everything around you will begin to order itself, and your Guiding Self will inform you of your next step.

This brings us to the second most important ingredient in Cosmic Creation, which is intuition. We define intuition as your ability to listen to your Guiding Self.

When I was a little girl, I received a fortune candle from my mother for my 10th birthday. The candle was in the shape of a pyramid and as it burned, charms inside the wax would fall out. One of these charms was a metal capsule and inside there was my fortune: "To listen well, is as powerful a means of influence as to talk well". A voice inside of me told me that this was very important, and so I kept it, and as a matter of fact, I still have that capsule today. I finally understand the capsule's message: To create your desire, you have to not only HEAR the Guiding Self but be OPEN to actually receiving the information and putting it into ACTION. This is true intuition.

With unconditional love comes the ability to trust, while fear brings doubt, and if doubt is present, you'll be unable to carry out the instructions or the blueprints for your desire. We will illustrate this with another story from the perspective of Amber.

One day, I woke up early to run, and as I began, I had an urge to run on the beach. I saw it as a quick picture in my mind of how beautiful the beach would be, and a feeling of wanting to be there. It all took place within a split second. Then, the voice of my Ego set in, "It will probably be too windy there, the wind is too cold, I won't go." Then I again had the thought to go to the beach, with an even stronger desire to go. I realized that my Guiding Self was talking to me and that this was part of an instruction. I was aware that my Guiding Self unconditionally loves me and that I am my Guiding Self. I am also aware that my Guiding Self can see beyond my human limitation. I heard my intuition and trusted it. I allowed my Guiding Self to inform my next action. I dropped the fear about the wind and went to the beach.

Doubt disconnects you from the ether, or the sphere of creation. Imagine this place like the internet, the Guiding Self as your Wi-Fi connection, and unconditional love as the password to your network. Without the code, you cannot connect and download what it is that you want to download.

At the beach, I found the weather to be beautiful and even warmer than near my house. This was the first part of the lesson.

We hear our Guiding Self in ideas, feelings, desires, and mental images. If past programming has conditioned you to doubt your internal world and only act upon external information, then you will forever turn away from the wisdom of your consciousness. You will never create your desire; never find your way home. We must learn to begin to trust our "inner voice" and act upon those instructions. Your Guiding Star Compass will help you in the beginning. Allow this infographic to help lead you in the direction of the star on the continuum of duality. After you receive an "instruction," ask yourself, "Will this action bring me towards my GSC coordinates? Will this action allow me to feel those feelings? Which ones?" Also, look at your new treatments and repeat the treatment you need to carry out this action. Ask yourself, "If I take this action, will it reinforce my treatment?" If your answers are yes, then take action, be grateful for the result, and send or feel love to and from your Guiding Self.

The lesson did not end there. At the beach, I saw a beautiful shell. My first instinct was to pick it up and put it into my pocket, but then my Guiding Self spoke to me again, not out loud, but in thoughts, ideas, images, and feelings. The Guiding Self told me that it was the Ego who told me to physically POSSESS the shell and to take it for my own. But what would I do with it? What was it that I really desired behind the physical shell? Which coordinate was this shell expressing for me? It was "beauty".

I was trying to possess beauty instead of expressing it or appreciating the shell's expression of beauty. The Guiding Self instructed me to enjoy its beauty within my heart, to love it, and stare in wonder at this perfect expression of beauty, a perfect expression of the Infinite. I thank the universe, touch the shell to my heart, and put it back. I left the beach with the beauty of that shell forever infused into every cell of my being. That beauty can never be lost, broken, or stolen. With the Guiding Self, there is no lack, only abundance. Thoughts of possession, taking, limitation, fear, and doubt are the language of the Ego. Thoughts of expression, freedom, unconditional love, and connection, are the Guiding Self's language. Be aware of the difference.

To listen to the Guiding Self, we must be aware of our connection to the universe and understand that unconditional love flows to us in every moment. You are deserving of your desire because you exist. You are deserving of love because you exist. When you come home to your soul, you are bathed in the eternal light of awareness. You can leave the darkness and chaos behind you and never look back, never re-animating the past. Even if you remember things, as we all do, you will now see them in the light of awareness, instead of in the darkness of ignorance and chaos. It is unconditional love for ourselves and all that exists that connects us to the frequency of the Infinite. It is only through love that we can become Cosmic Creators; welcome home.

Let us pick up where we left off in chapter 4, with the importance of unconditional love. Our ability to give and receive unconditional love reflects our relationship or "connection" to the Infinite, and the potentiality and possibility of our soul's expression. Unconditional love is accessed through the awareness that we are all one and that all separate bodies that we call humanity, plants, animals, minerals, etc. are pure illusion; a self-induced illusion to create infinite possibilities for expansion of consciousness. We are all nodes on a tree connected to one root. We are all one in the same, varying by degree or frequency. We call this the concept of **multiple experiences**.

We are one consciousness, expanding and expressing itself through multiple experiences. Space and time do not contain us, and therefore the Guiding Self (or your pool of consciousness) can be streaming into your body, your child's body, your siblings, your mother, and grandmother all at once. Reincarnation is not linear but simultaneous. This provides us with a new understanding of our interpersonal interactions. We begin to understand that we are interacting with ourselves. We are interacting with our own essence that has descended into a particular state of awareness. This is why and how our present actions affect the past, present, and future. We simultaneously stream into these places and times.

This is where unconditional love comes into play. When we realize that we are one entity and that separation is an illusion, we can begin to release judgment and honor one another's unique path. Each person is an integral part of creation. Without even one of us, reality as we know it falls apart. Understand that we are all one consciousness that has descended into different states and experiences. We are both the abuser and the abused. We are the perpetrator and the victim. We descend into delightful circumstances, and we descend into volatile circumstances.

There is no evil, only pieces of consciousness that have forgotten so deeply who they are, that they have become fused with the Ego. It all depends on how far we are located in relation to the frequency of unconditional love on the continuum of duality. This is why it is our sacred duty to follow our desires and express our essence. Through this action of expansion, you expand us all. Your light provides light for the entire tree. Your awareness helps all of consciousness to become more awake. When you shut down and limit your essence, you limit all of creation. It is through your expansion and expression that we all find salvation.

Understand the concept of multiple experiences, and you will drastically improve your experience here on earth. As you interact with each person in your daily life, silently send them love and see them in your mind's eye; loved, happy, growing, and achieving ease in any challenge or difficulty they have in their life. If they are being negative in their speech with you, critical, rude, or complaining, speak words of kindness and unconditional love in your mind. Focus on their higher qualities and speak about them in your mind and heart as you interact with them. To be conscious and aware takes great focus in the beginning because you're accustomed to another state of awareness.

We want to make the critical and vital point, that Cosmic Creation is not about running away from life, distancing yourself from "negative people", or those who are not as "awakened" as you are, because this is all an illusion. We are all one, and through these interactions, you will grow, expand, and become more aware. It is through these interactions that you will assist all of creation to expand. This is your mission.

Let us explain the energetics of negative interactions, and then we will walk you through one. Everyone is born into an environment that will cause them emotional wounds. These wounds are necessary to develop your unique personality and the right type of soil required to bring about a unique desired expression. When someone is triggered, it is because one of those Ego wounds have been touched to inspire a growth cycle. One has to be aware of multiple experiences and how it all works, to expand and grow from the wound.

When you say or do something that brings about a negative reaction or interaction from another, know that it is not you that they are angry with, because you are both one in the same. It is only the wound or "emotional button" of the Ego that triggers these feelings. Like the right mallet that strikes a gong to produce a certain sound, a particular ghost has been reawakened. Remember that the Ego has to vibrate at a slower/lower rate to anchor you into the "me", so this Ego-wound is vibrating in the frequency of perpetual wanting. The Ego perceives the world from that competitive mentality of lack because it vibrates so far from the frequency of unconditional love.

Because we still live in a state of spiritual amnesia, we begin to focus on the Ego and become enmeshed with it. We begin to believe that we are the Ego, and we begin to perceive the world through the lens of fear, lack, perpetual imperfection, and perpetual self-criticism. When someone is negative, depressed, or critical, they are under the misconception that they are the Ego; that is all. They get caught in the gravitational pull or the "black hole", and become consumed by the wound of imperfection. This causes a destructive fire inside, a creation of the Ego. Their Ego attempts to pass the destructive fire to you, because all energy seeks expansion and expression, wherever it falls on the continuum of duality.

Negative Interactions

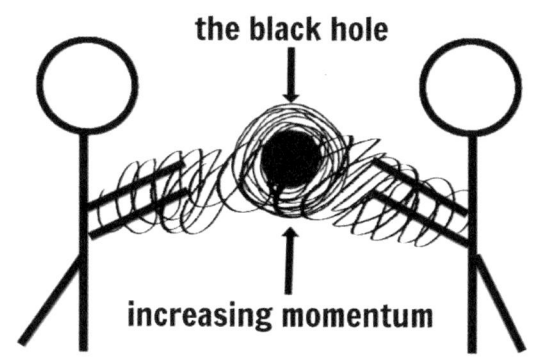

the black hole

increasing momentum

You accept the negativity into your energetic system and throw it back. Together you co-create a destructive force that continues to slow your rate of vibration. You move further away from the Guiding Self, away from creation and expansion, into destruction through limitation.

What usually happens is that you accept this fire, as your wound is "triggered". At this moment, you forget who you are and become caught in the gravitational pull of your Ego. As you accept this negative frequency, you allow yourself to vibrate at the rate of the other person, and this is why you get caught up in the Ego. It becomes like a game of catch, with a destructive fire building up after each pass. Together you create a black hole that sucks the light and vitality from both of you. Together you fall deeper into the hole, away from the Guiding Self and the energy of expansion. Together you increase the energy of destruction as you increase limitation through decreasing your awareness of who you are.

It is a mistake to run from life by trying to avoid confrontations. See these types of interactions as opportunities for the growth of all creation. See these experiences as your training ground. You're a warrior wielding the sword of unconditional love through your awareness of multiple experiences. You fight for growth, expansion, expression, and unconditional love for all of us. Instead of accepting and returning anger, hate, criticism, begin to return the opposite. Neutralize the fire and begin to grow the seeds of love and positivity in the "other". As you shift your focus to unconditional love, the Guiding Self speaks through you, and you remain in the frequency of creation, shining light that illuminates the darkness for all of us.

This can be difficult to figure out, so we will provide several common examples…

An argument with your family member or significant other:

In a romantic relationship, you and your partner get into a heated argument about any topic, to the point where your partner is calling you things such as: selfish, ridiculous, careless, or even stupid; basically, any words that appear to pass judgment on you. You are human, and you will become upset by this interaction. Remember that you are one consciousness, and it is the Ego now creating this perceived separation.

Step one: Remove yourself temporarily from the situation by going to another room, bathroom, or walking around the block. Let them know that you will be back but that you need a few minutes.

Step two: When you are alone, begin to whisper or say out loud the higher qualities of that person, remembering the concept of multiple experiences.

For example

1. You are so funny.
2. You are caring.
3. You are a loyal friend, etc…

Take deep breaths as you say these qualities

Please note: We are saying these qualities out loud because when the Ego is triggered, it begins to control your thoughts and your internal mind becomes like a stormy sea with thunder and lightning. If you remain there by attempting to speak the qualities in your mind, they will drown in the storm.

Step three: Begin to concentrate on the center of your chest by looking down at it as you breathe and continue to name the higher qualities of that person.

Step four: Feel the energy of unconditional love moving from your heart to your palms. Press your palms to the floor or together.

Step five: As you continue, change from naming the higher qualities to saying the pronoun "we" instead of the pronoun "you". We are connecting to the fact that we are one and diminishing the Ego's hold on us. For example,

    1. We are so funny
    2. We are caring
    3. We are loyal friends

Step six: Now begin to wish them wonderful things, they can be material things they want or emotional. This allows you to tap into the frequency of unconditional love. For example
    1. You feel so happy in your new house.
    2. You feel free and at ease.
    3. You are awakened to unconditional love.

Step seven: Now comes the step that will feel challenging at first, but will encourage your growth in consciousness and awareness. You return to the interaction and do so with the awareness that you're both expansive beings coming together to participate in an amazing opportunity for growth. It is through an imbalance that we seek balance, and it is out of the chaos that order is created. This is what you're here for. This seemingly negative interaction is actually your life classroom, and an opportunity for expansion and growth.

Step eight: Allow the other person to talk and release their frustrations as you listen. Breathe, concentrate on your heart, or the center of your chest and continue your positive wishes for them.

Step nine: Realize that the other person is upset because their Ego fears loss. Imagine their Guiding Self as a smiling version of them, and you both embrace. Ask their soul, "What is it that your Ego is fearing right now?"

Step ten: Trust the information coming to you, as your Guiding Self sees past the words coming out of their mouth, the words of the Ego. As you hear the answer, for example, "I don't matter", begin to breathe as you say in your now calm mind the opposite message, for example: "You matter because you are unconditionally loved."

Step eleven: We cannot tell you what to say during this type of interaction, but you will know what to do. Answer as needed out loud and in your mind. As they speak, continue to tell them (silently in your mind), the opposite of the limiting belief that is being played out by their Ego during this argument.

NEVER SAY any of the steps out loud or tell the other person that their Ego has possessed them. Doing so will only feed YOUR Ego and further agitate theirs. The goal of this exercise is to strengthen your ability to focus on unconditional love and strengthen your connection to the Guiding Self. Through these types of interactions, your ability to radiate light becomes stronger, and your creative power increases significantly. Energetically you have learned to "put out fires", and protect your energetic system from destructive energies that dim your light and drain your vitality. As a result, you will have contributed to all of creation with the radiance of your awareness; we all grow closer to the vibration of unconditional love.

Several words of caution: some individuals, as we have stated before, are fused with their Ego, since they have descended into a state that is very far from the awareness of unconditional love. In cases of physical violence, threats of violence, or emotional abuse, you must seek assistance from professionals and immediately remove yourself from danger. Never try to reenter physical space with someone who is violent or abusive. Remove yourself and practice steps one through ten in your mind, without physical contact, and then, as we did in chapter 2, walk out of this haunted house and do not return. In certain circumstances, individuals have created such a massive and dense black hole, that we must physically stay away from its gravitational pull. Abuse is one of those circumstances.

If no abuse is involved, and this is a regular argument or even a deep argument that results in not talking for a while with the other person, or they temporarily leave to get perspective, this is all okay. Continue to send love to you both and wishes of success and growth. Then, do not dwell on this, but go about your business. If fear comes up in any way, continue these practices and use your treatments throughout your day. Remember that you are never alone, and that imbalance is an opportunity for creation and growth. Remember who and what you truly are.

Negative interactions at work/Complaining:

Most negative interactions at work are not as triggering as those from home, so they may take less concentration and focus, as the intensity is less. If a coworker begins complaining to you about the job, the boss, the building, etc., listen to the fear behind the complaint. Name their higher qualities in your mind, feel your heart, and tell them the opposite of their complaints in your mind.

For example:
"Can you believe this new project? They're asking too much of us."
I hear: Overwhelm and frustration.
I say in my mind: "You are free and feel the joy and relief of your freedom. You're peaceful and relaxed."

Then change to we:
"We are free and feel the joy and relief of our freedom. We are peaceful and relaxed."
Continue concentrating on the center of your chest and notice any interesting sensations there.

Do not run away from or try to avoid these interactions. The Guiding Self, our true essence is about expansion and expression. Do not hide from life but engage with it. See life as a playground on which we play games, laugh, run, feel free, fall down, scrape a knee, or get into a fight. All of these experiences are opportunities to increase our awareness and expand all of consciousness. The only way to accomplish this is to have the right perspective, so that you can see the opportunities for growth. The platform that gives you this perspective is unconditional love.

Seek to connect to this free-flowing power in every circumstance. Creation is a delicate balance of formation and disintegration, anabolism, and catabolism. Destruction is fire, and formation is water. When we feed destruction, it grows and produces a consuming void, a heavy, slow vibrating mass that conceals light but appears as if it consumes the light. When you water seeds of positivity with unconditional love, you begin to release the mass, dissolve it, and the light begins to emerge once again.

Much of our conditioning and modes of operation come from verbal language. Language itself is a limited form of communication because it places limits on what you're able to express. Your collective language reflects your collective current state of consciousness on planet Earth. We must do our best to explain concepts that are not currently supported by the earthly language. This is why we combine these words with visuals such as the dreams we have presented to convey something deeper that moves beyond language. It is helpful to be aware that you were limited and subconsciously shaped by the politics of your earthly language.

Let us explain how insidious language can be. Language is a veil that limits our view and has been created by our collective focus or state of awareness. We are the "deceptors" of ourselves. Words carry intentions and meanings at their core and produce a certain frequency during their utterance. The English word "compassion" is one of the most dangerous words in the English language. Compassion is often used, praised, and encouraged. But hidden at its core is a meaning conveyed almost subliminally, a meaning that veils your awareness and hinders your energetic growth.

Compassion is the word that speaks of pain, misery, and sorrow. Like a spell, it commands you to focus on the pain of another and water the seeds of misery, just as we observed during the examples of negative interactions. As we water the seeds of pain in the other, we water those same seeds in ourselves. The seeds grow and generate pulses of misery that dim your light of awareness and the awareness of all consciousness. Instead, water the seeds of happiness. Seek them out in others by becoming aware of their Ego fears and subconscious patterns that lead them down roads of chaos and pain. Through the lens of unconditional love, send them back the treatments for those fears as you engage with their soul and not with their Ego. We would call this concept "conjoyment", instead of compassion, as you connect with another soul's joy and not the perceived pain and loss perpetuated by the Ego.

Our language evolves, as it is a series of audible projections that form out of our current state of awareness. We are moving from the fearing- wanting of the Ego, towards the loving-desiring of the soul or Guiding Self. Our purpose and desire is to encourage the fullness of your spirit to radiate and express itself outward into physical reality. Your essence is that of the Infinite. All are good in origin because every soul/point of consciousness vibrates at the frequency of unconditional love. Anything else is contrary to your true nature.

When we commiserate with another or focus on their misery, we are both focusing contrary to our true consciousness. We begin to focus through the lens of the Ego-wanting and, as a result, amplify the vibration of negativity throughout all consciousness. These negative waves or disturbances throughout the subtle-energetic realms build in momentum. The waves create a magnetic field or gravitational pull that begins to attract like energies toward it, building momentum like a snowball growing larger as it rolls down a hill. The waves finally slow down and solidify into physical matter. This is how we co-create negativity. The reverse is also true, and much more powerful because it is through unconditional love that we connect to our true essence, (the Guiding Self) and set the energetic world ablaze with our light. Like a supernova, we fill all of creation with our light. These positive waves build in momentum and filter down into physical matter as physical experiences and results.

These practices take time, and they are part of a greater process of expanding your awareness as you engage in conscious living. There will be some interactions where you carry these instructions out perfectly and walk away feeling wonderful. There will be other times when you cannot see beyond your Ego because the gravitational pull is too strong. This is totally normal, and it is all an individual process without perfection. There is no ending point to expansion and no rubric for judgment.

Our message is to engage with life consciously to expand your awareness and, therefore, your ability to express your soul. Engage with the life that you created, don't run away from it. This process does not involve actively eliminating people from your life or pushing negative thoughts away. Conscious living means engaging with everything and everyone in the pursuit of greater awareness by taking the perspective of unconditional love.

We have the ability to shift our focus and change perspective so that we can experience the majesty all around us. We define "free will" as your ability to choose your focus. Focus affects the depth of your awareness and your ability to see opportunities that are available to you. Everything you need to expand is right in your living room or your immediate environment. Take the time to grow the frequencies for the seeds of positivity that you desire. Your current life and circumstances are the right soil needed to grow your desires. Never wish for someone else's life because you chose the specific environment needed to bring all of your desires into fruition.

"We are one consciousness, expanding and expressing itself through multiple experiences"

~Lavender Moon

---

6 THE SPIRITUAL MOUTH
ACTIVATING OUR ENERGETIC WOMB

In real life...

I'm 30 years old, and I'm lying on the floor with my chest supported by a bolster in a modified yoga pose called "fish". There are blankets draped over me. I have been in this posture for nearly 45 minutes and feeling very impatient. Finally, our teacher tells us that it is time to switch with our partners, and I feel relieved. I am in the mountains of Utuado in Puerto Rico, attending yoga teacher training. Our teacher is leading myself and about ten other women through a partner exercise where one partner breathes deeply in the modified fish pose, while the other examines where in their body that breath is obstructed or not working to its fullest potential.*

I am excited because it is my turn to sit up and examine my partner's posture. But, there is an odd number of students. "Amber will go again," says our teacher. "You mean I have to do that again for another 45 minutes?" I say in disbelief. "Yes," she says. I am switched to a new partner, and down I go again, onto the bolster. After about 20 minutes, something strange begins to happen. I begin to breathe very deeply, so deeply that I think my upper back is lifting slightly off of the bolster. Is this possible? How high is my back arched? A strange feeling begins to bloom in my chest, and the sensation of electricity begins to intensify at the center of my chest.

The feeling is so intense that I become scared. I try to move, but it hurts my body. Something tells me just to let go. I relax, and the pain disappears, but it feels like bolts of electricity are being pumped through my body. The electricity moves from my chest through the palms of my hands. The feeling is so intense I feel like I might explode. The more I relax, the more intense the feeling is, but there is no pain. If I try to move, it hurts, and suddenly I have no control over my body. My fingers stiffen and begin to twist around the invisible bolts of lightning that are shooting out from or into my palms, I can't tell.

I hear a voice in my mind, "Don't be afraid. Let go and open your heart." I completely relax, and I feel as if I'm lifting up out of my body. No more pain. My back dissolves, and I'm surrounded by blackness...no, black water. I am peering out of the water as if I'm standing in water up to the bridge of my nose, so that only my eyes and the top of my head are above water. I'm staring into the eyes of a great crocodile whose eyes are peering out of the blackness in the same way. We are inches from one another, and something I can't explain happens like there's one part of my brain that tells me that this is not a good situation, but the fear dissolves, and love suddenly fills my being. As she opens her massive jaws to me the word "mother" unexpectedly fills my mind and I crawl inside her mouth, into the darkness once again.

A dim light begins to brighten, and I'm standing on the ground somewhere. It is night. I don't know how I know, but I know, and I understand that I'm in a pyramid. I am flanked by priests to my right and to my left in a line. Their heads are shaved, and they wear white. I seem much taller than them. I stand with my arms outstretched, and they seem delicate and small next to me. In the blackness, I see a large snake. Are we the same size? We look into each other's eyes...a large hawk or eagle...and then I'm snapped back down into my body by my partner's hands on me, trying to roll me onto my side as the teacher instructs.

Our teacher calls us to the circle so we can share our experiences. I try very hard to come back, but my entire body is shaking. I try to regain control, but I can't. I make my way into the circle and sit next to my roommate during this retreat. "What's wrong?" she asks. "I dddon't knnoow," I say shakily, as I press the palms of my hands into the ground, trying unsuccessfully to stop the shaking. My hands are still cupped as if twisting around a ball. The feeling of electricity isn't stopping. I suddenly raise my hand, "Something is wrong," and I lift up my hands as I continue to shake.

The next thing I know, my head is on the teacher's lap, I think. As I breathe and relax, the electricity intensifies, and I suddenly wonder if I will survive this, or will I explode? Everyone in the room has their hands on me. They're trying to ground me. I hear our teacher instructing me to yell or scream, to "let it out." My mouth opens, but I'm no longer in control. I feel people trying to straighten my palms. My mouth forms the shape of an "O", and I begin to omit a deep "ohhhhhhh" sound. I'm hearing this, but it's as if it isn't me, and I'm shocked by the sound that I hear and then...blackness. In a split-second, I am as big as a mountain. I don't know what I am. I have the head of the lion. I open my arms and in front of me IS a mountain. I am filled with electrical power. I can crush this mountain into pieces. I feel intoxicated by this power.

Our teacher is lifting me up, "Get her up," she says. They're taking me outside and walking me straight into the pool. It stops, but I'm still shaking. Our teacher places me wet on the concrete to lie down. Every muscle in my body is sore, and it feels as if someone is pressing me with their finger right between my eyes. This doesn't go away for hours. That evening, as I walk back to my cottage, a small owl flies over to me and lands on a branch a few feet away. At first, I think, "how cute," but as I move closer, it doesn't fly away. It just looks at me. I'm standing with my face inches from its face now. It turns its head sideways the way owls do and looks right at me. Suddenly, I'm unnerved, and a bit "weirded-out" and I walk away.

In my room, my roommate and I settle down to sleep. I'm still trying to process what happened earlier that day. When I turn my body to face the window by my bed, I'm facing a neon–green ball of light on the shade. "Andie?" "Yeah," she answers in a tired voice. "Do you see this?" We both sit up scared because we think it must be a weird, large lightning bug in Puerto Rico, or someone is playing a trick on us. The latter is more than scary because it's very late and we're in the middle of the forest. I look out from under the shade, and I see nothing. The light is now in our room. "Someone must be using a laser light," I say. "Through the shade AND the curtains?" Andy asks. "Yeah...maybe," I say, trying to convince myself. I make sure that the door is locked, and eventually, we go to sleep.

I wake up around 3:30 AM, and as I open my eyes, I see a dim, white sphere hovering about 6 inches from my face. I'm used to this. It's nothing new. I've seen these my whole life. "Go away," I say out loud, and I watch it fly away into the wall behind me, followed by a smaller one. I'm used to these...what do they call it? Hypnagogic hallucinations, that's it. I turn around and go back to sleep. In a few days, I fly back home, and over time, I forget...

I'm 33 years old, and my friend asks if I will be a guest yoga teacher at a safe house for young women who have survived sexual exploitation. What else can I do but say yes? But I'm very nervous. I walk in, and something seems to take over. I begin to feel a softer version of what I felt in the mountains of Utuado. It feels almost like butterflies in my chest and warmth spreading through my hands. I begin speaking, and I don't even know what I'm saying because I don't know which words are coming next, but they keep coming. I feel stronger with a great power moving through my chest.

I see a girl turn off her cellphone, and two others stop talking, and then they are all listening to me. I don't know how I am doing this. I lead them through the class. By the end, one of the girls is crying, and she says, "Thank you." I hug her, and this feeling in my chest like heat, like unconditional love to the hundredth power, fills my heart all the way up to between my eyebrows. As I walk to the subway, I say to myself, "What is this feeling? It feels like heaven. If only I could feel like this every day." I travel home, beaming with love and joy. That night at around 3:30 AM, I wake up to the usual. "Go away," I say out loud. The white sphere floats up through the ceiling over my bed. I turn over and go to sleep. Time passes, and I forget...

I'm 38 years old, and I'm in my office at work. I get to work very early, and so I'm the only one there. The lights are still off, and I'm frantic because I keep getting this intense feeling in my chest for no reason. It moves up to the space between my eyebrows and crisscrosses across the bridge of my nose to the top of my cheekbones on each side of my face. I feel it through my hands very intensely. I've had every blood test and scan possible. "What is happening to me?" I say out loud. "I get this feeling, but what am I supposed to do with this? What do I do with my hands? Am I a healer? Do I put my hands on people and heal them?" This doesn't feel quite right. "What is my purpose, anyway?! What's the whole point, or is there none?!" This time I don't forget. Like a bolt of lightning, I remember, I remember everything, and I know exactly what to do. I pick up a pen, and I write, and I write, and I write...

We're naturally resonant beings, meaning that our mind-body machine is built to house our unique state of consciousness as human beings. Our physical bodies are constructed in a way that allows us to operate energetically, while remaining in physical form. We're designed to receive and broadcast or radiate energy in the form of frequency. As we live in a state of amnesia due to our incarnation or fusion with the Ego, we have forgotten how to use a vital energetic, and physical organ that we called the **spiritual mouth**. Your spiritual mouth can be seen as an energetic womb that we all possess, regardless of our mind-body machine's sex. The spiritual mouth is the key organ used in the Art of Cosmic Creation by enabling us to communicate with the Guiding Self and translate our desires into physical reality.

Let us explain precisely how the spiritual mouth works. The Guiding Self streams into the center of the chest at the cardiac plexus. Imagine that you are placing your pointer finger into the center of a bowl, where you represent the Guiding Self, and the bowl represents your mind-body machine. Your finger represents the partial self or the part of you that fills the bowl with your presence. The point where your finger comes into contact with the bowl is the spiritual mouth. The Ego can be seen as a type of glue that would adhere your finger to the bowl so that the finger and YOU would not lose contact with the bowl. However, the glue (as all things physical are), is temporary and will eventually come apart. This event is what you call death. While the finger is connected to the bowl, it.thinks that all it is, is a bowl, or it may be aware that it is a finger in a bowl, but it has forgotten that it is attached to a vast being that is all of YOU, the Guiding Self.

The point where your physical body is animated by your soul, is at the center of your chest or your spiritual mouth. This is where the Guiding Self sends frequency into your body or energetic impulses carrying information like electricity moving through wires. These impulses or frequencies carry the seeds to your expansion. They are your desires or your soul's blueprints for evolution. The energy fills your chest cavity and moves upwards through your throat and into your sinus cavity. These two sets of cavities act as one resonance chamber that amplifies and focuses vibration. The brain acts as a receiver. The brain picks up the frequency and interprets it into mental pictures that produce feelings. In other words, the brain receives the code from your Guiding Self and interprets the information in a way that the mind-body machine can understand. The mind-body machine operates based on the language of feeling through emotions and physical sensations. The spiritual mouth is where your body connects with your soul, and your brain is the translator between the body and the soul, the Guiding Self, and the Partial Self. Like the force of gravity within a star, this is the force of attraction. It is the inward pull of something desiring to be expressed by the Guiding Self.

The Spiritual Mouth

Messages/coordinates in the form of vibration from The Guiding Self are projected into the Spiritual Mouth. The frequencies are amplified and guided upward by the resonance chamber to the brain. The messages are received by the brain and converted into pictures, ideas, and concepts.

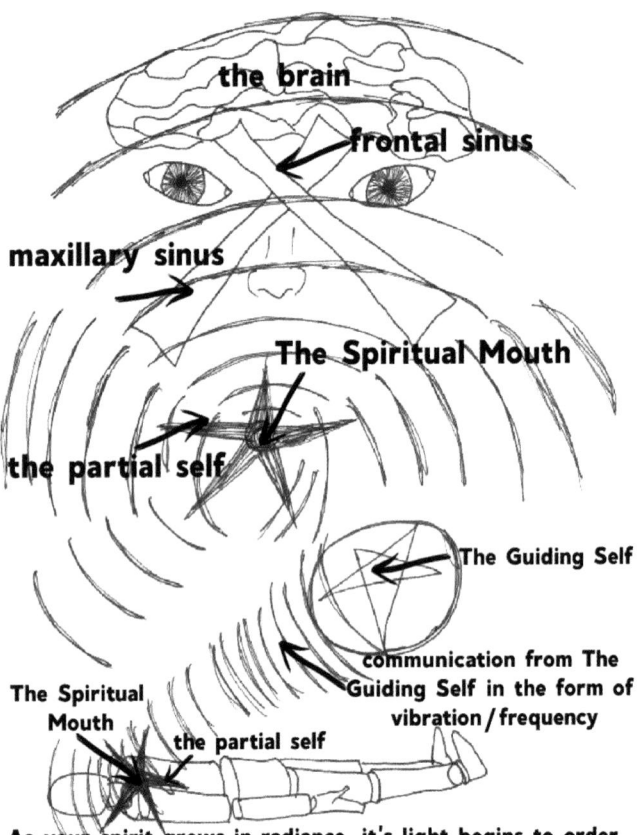

- the brain
- frontal sinus
- maxillary sinus
- The Spiritual Mouth
- the partial self
- The Guiding Self
- communication from The Guiding Self in the form of vibration / frequency
- The Spiritual Mouth
- the partial self

As your spirit grows in radiance, it's light begins to order your physical reality through the expression of your desire

There is a second part to this process, where the direction or force that is opposite to expression, projections, fusion, and radiation occurs. The conscious mind and the subconscious mind (the subconscious mind operates the body and carries the operating software installed into your body) interact. Remember that your soul or Guiding Self has chosen your exact environment and childhood, needed to create the right soil to germinate your seeds of expansion and awareness. The subconscious and Ego are connected as they directly govern the body and work together to keep your consciousness separate so that all consciousness can expand in infinite ways and express infinite potential.

The Guiding Self provides the raw material for the blueprint, but the conscious and subconscious minds work together to further define the structure of what will ultimately be produced. The original frequency or information received will be altered, defined, structured, and the resulting frequency will be projected back outward into physical reality. In other words, the subconscious tempers what is sent down or poured down from the Infinite. How much you project from the Guiding Self's desires versus the Ego's wants is called **radiation**. This is what we define as true power. Now you can understand why it is so important to align the subconscious mind with the direction of the Guiding Self. In this way, more of your true self will shine through.

Once again, being aware of the function of the Ego will help you let go of the limitations that its agent, FEAR, would normally hold over you. Being aware of this entire process helps you to understand who and what you are, and this is the foundation that you are using to build the physical representation of your desires. The spiritual mouth is the key to co-creation with the Guiding Self because it's the place where you physically connect, or your point of contact. Your physical body was designed to accommodate this connection and this function of the spiritual mouth. The purpose of a resonance chamber is to focus and amplify waves of energy. This is exactly what your body does, and is constructed for; to accommodate the conjunction of the mind-body machine, and the Guiding Self. As we have said, "we are naturally resonant beings", and this is how we receive information and communicate with the world around us; through vibration and frequency.

There are two forces or directions of creation. One direction moves towards integration and expansion. The other direction moves towards disintegration and limitation. These two forces work in tandem to maintain balance, just like the forces of gravity and fusion in a star, or the forces of electricity and magnetism in an atom, or like the forces of action and attraction in manifestation. It is all the same. Like a question and an answer. The Guiding Self is held in physical reality, and your consciousness is anchored and "separated" by the Ego. All things in physical reality work through this push and pull on the continuum of duality. We can see the concept of frequency and resonance in the same way.

Resonance can be seen as a vibrational connection between two sources of frequency. Resonance happens when two frequencies meet in harmony and complement each other to produce something more powerful than they could have on their own, like a symphony. The more we project and receive vibrations or feelings aligned with the Guiding Self, the stronger we radiate our electromagnetic energy or light outward, like a star. You can imagine the rays of light that project outward from your spiritual mouth like tentacles seeking more vibrations that are in resonance with the Guiding Self, the very feelings that you have written into your Guiding Star Compass. The more you radiate outward from the spiritual mouth as a result of the partial self and Guiding Self, working together in harmony, the more you will produce and attract the building blocks of your desires. This is all accomplished by activating and working through your spiritual mouth, your long-forgotten energetic/physical organ of creation; the nucleus of your star.

Resonance, like everything in physical reality, operates on the continuum of duality. You can choose to move in either direction along the continuum by generating and attracting vibrations that are in resonance with the rate of vibration generated by the Guiding Self, or the rate of vibration generated by the Ego. When you focus on feeling and producing the feelings written in your GSC, we call this "positive resonance". When you focus on feeling and producing feelings of fear, anger, doubts, etc., we call this "negative resonance". Negative resonance moves you towards the void of the black hole, and you begin to vibrate from the Ego and attract limitation into your physical experience. In this case, you are in "dissonance" with the Guiding Self, producing a cacophony of vibration, like what you call chaos, the opposite of a symphony.

As we have said, the spiritual mouth is both an energetic and physical organ, which means it is felt physically and not just a mental concept. The spiritual mouth is felt most strongly as a sensation at a point in the center of the chest, and a point between the eyebrows that radiates down the sides of the bridge of your nose, in the direction of your cheekbones. As its intensity grows or wanes, the sensations will be different. You may feel the sensation radiate down your arms towards the center of your palms or from the bridge of your nose to your cheeks. You may feel a heat-like sensation along your face. In the beginning, you may only feel the center of your chest or only the point between your eyebrows or only the bridge of your nose. You may even experience intense headaches in the beginning. This is all part of the awakening process because an organ that has not been used before is waking up.

Imagine this process as if someone tied one arm to the trunk of your body when you were born, so you never moved your arm, and operated your whole life with one arm. You were never conscious of the other arm and never knew its potential, or were even aware of the sensation of having two arms. You were unaware of your capability for having two arms. Then, one day, someone took the binding off. At first, the sensation would be strange, maybe even scary, and uncomfortable. The arm would be weak, and you may not even be able to control it very well at first. It may ache when activated, but over time you would develop its strength and gain the ability to use two arms and hands. Your potential would be realized, and the same is true with the spiritual mouth.

Just as positive residence can be felt in the above-described regions of the body, so can negative resonance. Recall the continuum of duality where the Guiding Self and the star of creation and expansion are located at the top and the Ego, and the black hole of limitation are located at the bottom. The same goes for the sensations in the body. Remember that vibration is felt and not seen. Just as vibration can be detected by emotional feelings, they can also be detected by physical sensations. These are the two ways that you experience vibration or detect various frequencies on a daily basis. When you are in harmony with the Guiding Self, positive resonance can be felt in the center of your chest and upward. Negative resonance can be felt anywhere below the chest, such as sensations in the stomach. These lower sensations indicate that you are moving in the opposite direction of your desires or your GSC. You are moving towards limitation and possession, and away from expansion and expression.

The Continuum and The Mind-Body Machine

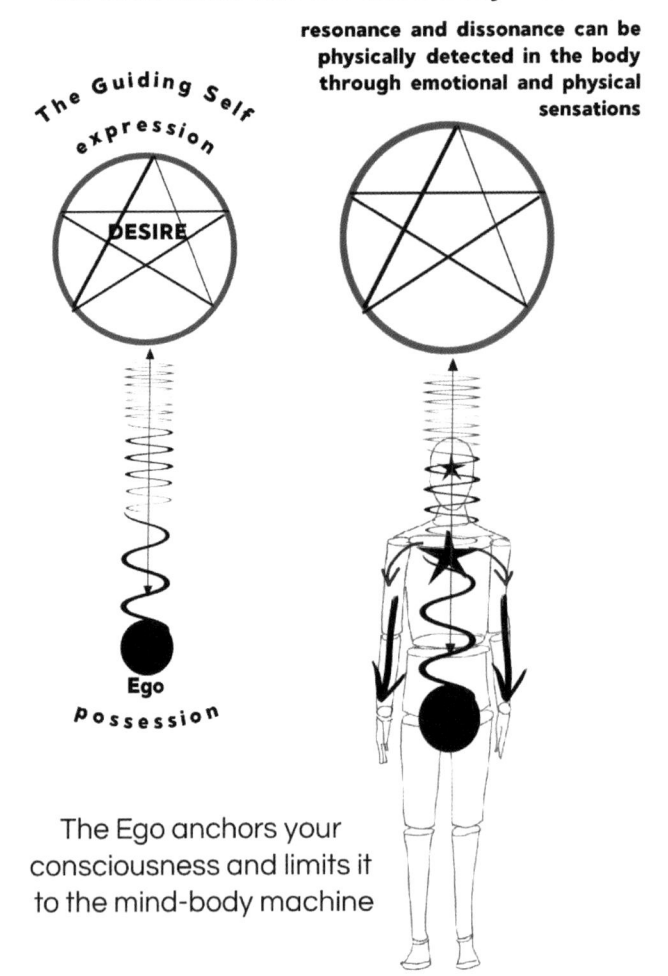

The Guiding Self

expression

DESIRE

resonance and dissonance can be physically detected in the body through emotional and physical sensations

Ego

possession

The Ego anchors your consciousness and limits it to the mind-body machine

Different bodies are designed to hold different states of consciousness. A shark's body is very different from the human body. When consciousness enters a body, it slows down and is anchored into the body by the Ego. Ego, as we have explained, is the glue that binds the soul to the body. The Ego is connected to what you call "the reptilian brain" and is concerned with the body or survival of the mind-body machine, and limitation of consciousness. The Ego is the necessary counterbalance needed to experience physical reality. The Ego is the vehicle through which we can accomplish infinite expansion of infinite potential. When the soul is bound to the body, imagine a slinky toy that has been stretched out so that it now fills your body. Your partial self streams in through the heart/center of your chest and slows down or stretches out to fill the physical vehicle.

The concept of "chakras" or "energy centers" comes into play here. When your consciousness is "stretched out" or extended, a "separation" or "differentiation" or "filtering down" begins to occur (as seen in the accompanying picture). This process is very disorienting to our consciousness and is the reason we become unaware of who and what we are. This process creates a veil that hides us from seeing our own identity. The physical vehicle is chosen to house or embody different states of consciousness.

You Are a Star of Creation

consciousness

Think of consciousness as white light that contains all of the colors in the electromagnetic spectrum.

Imagine the spectrum in this undifferentiated state as a slinky coiled tightly into a circle.

white light

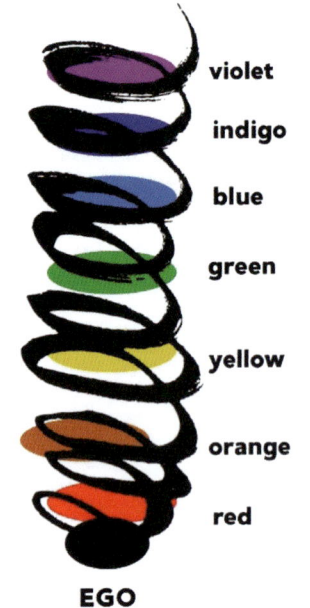

- violet
- indigo
- blue
- green
- yellow
- orange
- red

EGO

The slinky extends and opens, stretching and differentiating.

The differentiation of consciousness occurs as each portion of consciousness is "separated" or differentiated by frequency into each color on the electromagnetic spectrum.

Let us look at the energetic anatomy of a shark versus the human. Notice the difference between the "coils of consciousness" in the human and in the shark. The difference is in the spiritual mouth or the place where they radiate outward. If we look at what most of the world has come to recognize as chakras, (the places where the coil of consciousness differentiates and separates) they are actually points where the frequency of that coil "filters down", and "drops" in its rate or frequency to accommodate that mind-body machine. The way in which the coil filters down reflects our state of consciousness.

The specific mind-body machine calls for that state of consciousness, and consciousness calls for the right mind-body machine. In the human body, we are designed to radiate outward from the chest or our "heart", primarily, which extends upward to the brain. In other words, you can detect or experience frequencies as emotional feelings. Humans are at the level of consciousness, where you have the ability to understand your true identity and connection to ALL, while simultaneously streaming into a mind-body machine.

The Coils of Consciousness in Humans vs Sharks

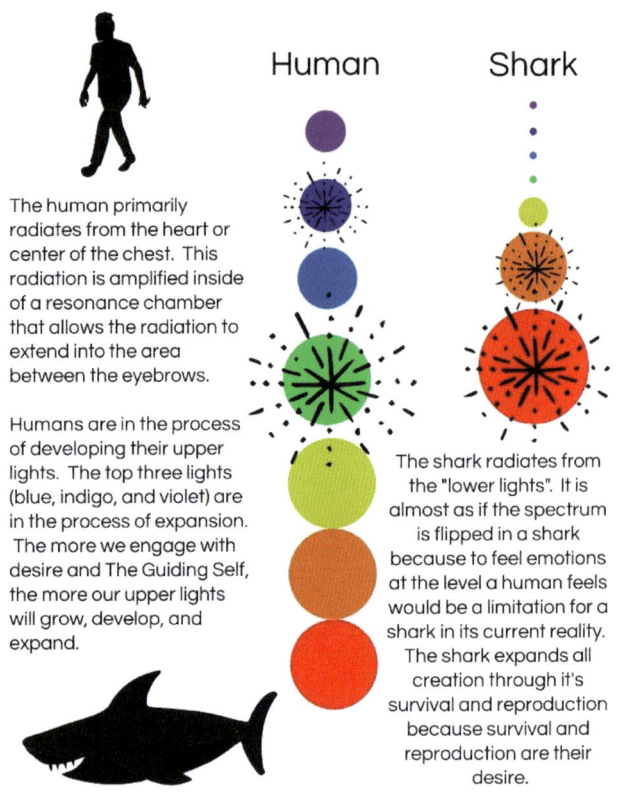

Human

Shark

The human primarily radiates from the heart or center of the chest. This radiation is amplified inside of a resonance chamber that allows the radiation to extend into the area between the eyebrows.

Humans are in the process of developing their upper lights. The top three lights (blue, indigo, and violet) are in the process of expansion. The more we engage with desire and The Guiding Self, the more our upper lights will grow, develop, and expand.

The shark radiates from the "lower lights". It is almost as if the spectrum is flipped in a shark because to feel emotions at the level a human feels would be a limitation for a shark in its current reality. The shark expands all creation through it's survival and reproduction because survival and reproduction are their desire.

The Shark: The dominance and "heaviness" of the lower lights in comparison to the upper lights create a side to side movement of the spine in reptiles as opposed to the forward and back movement of a mammal's spine which is due to the expansion of the upper lights that begins in the heart or center of the chest.

The coil of consciousness in the body of a shark radiates outward from the red and orange centers. These centers are closer to the Ego or "glue" on the spectrum of duality. The shark is experiencing a state of consciousness that is focused on physical survival and reproduction. The "upper lights" are yet undeveloped, and their radiation from these upper lights are but specs of dust. We are all one consciousness, but we experience different states, and our mind-body machines are built to accommodate these various states of consciousness. The shark exists between the "level of entry" and "the level of self".

In a human body, your coil of consciousness has the ability to reach the level of Cosmic Creation by becoming aware of the Guiding Self and, therefore, to consciously direct the frequencies you choose to receive and project. This is how we consciously create our experience in the physical realm. We accomplish all of this through the spiritual mouth.

Exercise Six–Opening the Spiritual Mouth

As you will soon see, the spiritual mouth is critical in both transmitting and pulling your vision/desires into physical reality. This is the place where we perceive guidance from the Guiding Self and pull in the vibrations we need to carry out our vision. The spiritual mouth energetically mirrors and acts as a physical womb. This is the place where we energetically incubate and grow our vision. Before we can accomplish this, we need to physically regain sensation of the spiritual mouth, and strengthen it as you would any muscle. We will give you three methods to practice. The goal is to eventually be able to open the spiritual mouth and bring on the sensations at will, within seconds, just as you would be able to speak, using your physical vocal cords. Eventually, we can let go of these exercises.

Method One: Using Your Treatments

Because your treatments are directly connected to the language or vibration of your spirit, (unconditional love), the same vibrations/feelings produced by the treatments stimulate the spiritual mouth.

Step One: Setting the Stage

Sit down comfortably on the couch. Make sure there is nothing constricting or blocking your chest, like a bra or even any type of necklace. It is helpful to remove all jewelry and even socks to allow the energy to flow without constriction. Wear comfortable, loose-fitting clothing. Your legs may be folded or cross-legged, or straight in front of you. Comfort is key here. Allow yourself to lean onto your headboard if you are in your bed, or relax back onto your couch. Wherever you are, make sure that your back is supported. Place a pillow behind you so your chest is open outward and not crunched inward. A blanket is also helpful on your legs for comfort and warmth.

Step Two: Release Mental Grasping and Breathe

Close your eyes and begin to breathe deeply. Feel the breath expand your body from your belly to your chest. Breathe in and out slowly through the nostrils only. Do this for ten deep breaths. If anything comes to your mind, say within yourself, "I release all mental grasping and radiate from my Guiding Self," Allow your body to relax.

Step Three: The Wheel

Imagine a boat's nautical steering wheel. Imagine one small enough to fit inside of your chest. Imagine placing this wheel inside of your chest, right between the pectoral muscles. Focus on the wheel in your chest and continue breathing into it. Can you feel the sensation there? Perhaps you feel a slight "pressing" between the eyebrows? Continue to breathe like this for ten deep breaths and notice any physical sensations in the chest, between the eyebrows, or ringing in the ears.

Step Four: Raising the Energy

Now continue seeing the wheel in your chest. As you breathe, feel the air moving from the wheel in your chest, continuing up your throat, and up through your nose, to the bridge of your nose, all the way to the space between your eyebrows. Continue this for five deep breaths. Notice any physical sensations in either area as you breathe.

Step Five: Resonating and Radiating

Now you can open your eyes and begin reading your first treatment. Try to repeat your treatment or "feel it" with your eyes closed. Imagine the wheel in your chest dissolving into light, until it becomes a star in the center of your chest. As you breathe in slowly and deeply, mentally recite your first treatment, and as you do, imagine on your next inhale, the light of your star becoming brighter so that its rays of light extend further outward from your body in all directions. Imagine that the treatment is feeding the star strength and the breath brings this treatment into the star.

On the exhale, your star radiates further and brighter. Feel the light extend through the throat upward and outward from between your eyebrows, like a second smaller star. Concentrate on the physical feelings this produces and repeat with all treatments.

Slowly, open your eyes and become aware of how you feel physically.

Note: This will take time in the beginning, but over time it will become easier. The key is to focus on the physical sensations this exercise produces in your chest and upward to your sinus cavities. This allows your body and brain to recognize and remember how to open the spiritual mouth physically. Eventually, you will no longer need this exercise to access the spiritual mouth.

Method Two: Walking with Gratitude

Real gratitude can be experienced physically. These exercises are about re-training you to physically feel frequencies and vibrations so that your spirit can work together with your mind-body machine. Real gratitude is not about thinking but feeling. This exercise is done while walking outside. This exercise is best completed in an area with nature. If you're in the city try to find a park. Even a small one will do.

Step One: Setting the Stage

As you walk, make sure that you're comfortable and that nothing is constricting your chest or rib cage. Do not wear any jewelry on your body.

Step Two: Release Mental Grasping and Breathe

Just as with method one, begin to breathe deeply from your belly to your chest. Release all mental grasping. If any thoughts come to mind, say to yourself, "I release all mental grasping. I don't have to worry about that now." Continue to concentrate on your breath. Feel your body becoming relaxed and invigorated.

Step Three: The Wheel

In your mind's eye, picture the nautical wheel inside of your chest. Feel it there as you breathe deeply and walk. Feel the vitality growing in your body.

Step Four: Raising the Energy

As you continue to imagine and feel the wheel in your chest, feel the cool air moving into your nostrils and upward towards the space between your eyebrows. Imagine and feel a small wooden wheel between the eyebrows were two of the lower spokes fit on either side of the bridge of your nose. Try to feel the point between your eyebrows where the wheel is embedded, and the spokes at the bridge of your nose.

Step Five: Connect the Dots

As you breathe deeply and slowly, bring your attention to all three areas. Feel the wheel in your chest, the wheel between the eyebrows, and on the right and left sides, on the bridge of your nose. Try to feel these three areas physically, you may experience a heat-like sensation on your cheeks; this is normal. Practice these sensations for ten deep breaths.

Step Six: Gratitude

Try to maintain the physical sensations and breathe deeply, as you practice this next step. Now begin to look and listen around you. This is an example: Notice the trees and the leaves. Notice the beautiful emerald color of the leaves. Focus on it with gratitude and awe as you take a deep breath and feel the spiritual mouth taking that beauty into you. As you "light up", the tree lights up as well energetically, because you are connected. Feel the connection with the spiritual mouth and breathe in almost as if you were drinking the object of focus into you. Notice the beauty all around you as you walk, the trees, grass, flowers, sky, animals, insects, and the sounds of nature. Delight in all of these things and drink them into you by focusing on them, breathing in deeply and simultaneously feeling the physical sensations of the heart, the point between the eyebrows, and along the sides of the bridge of the nose. This is real gratitude, the physical, emotional, and energetic experience of connecting on a vibrational level with creation. This act infuses your body with vitality and brings vitality to all creation. This is your true language. You are a resonant being.

Walking with Gratitude

Breathe and release all
mental grasping

Feel the wheel within and use it to steer and guide the direction of your life, always moving towards your desire along the continuum of duality.

Method Three: Watering the Seeds of Positivity

You can access the vibration of joy in anyone and anything. This particular exercise will help you to strengthen your ability to communicate and form positive relationships with other human beings. This exercise will also strengthen your ability to transform negative interactions into positive ones, as discussed in Chapter 5. This method is best carried out in public places where you have access to many different people such as on a bus, train, subway, or Café. It works best to be seated during this exercise.

Step One: Access the Spiritual Mouth

Sit in a place where you can remain undisturbed while being surrounded by people. Public transport works best, especially for long rides. Access the spiritual mouth by breathing, picturing the wheel at the heart, and the eyebrows. Try to simultaneously feel all three areas of the spiritual mouth; the center of chest, the point between the eyebrows, and the sides along the bridge of the nose. Take 5 to 10 deep breaths to deepen and magnify these sensations.

Step Two: Focus on the Physical

Bring your attention to a person. Glance at them so you can see them and then look away. Please do not stare at people because they will be offended. Simply glance and then hold their image in your imagination, sitting there. You may close your eyes or leave them open. Listening to inspiring music on your headphones can also help the process.

Step Three: Water the Seeds of Positivity

With the spiritual mouth open (which means you can physically feel part or all of it), imagine the person smiling and feeling so much joy. Just as you did with the tree in nature, begin to drink this joy in as you breathe in and access their joy. Feel yourself drinking/breathing in their joy and laughter through the spiritual mouth. Feel your body becoming infused with that joy until it hums with the vibration of joy and happiness. Remember that as you do this, you're simultaneously watering the seeds of joy in them because you are connected. As you light up, they light up.

Step Four: Continue

Repeat this process with as many people as you can for the duration of your ride. You may notice them begin to smile or notice people already smiling, or talking with others and laughing. Amplify their joy by drinking it all in through the spiritual mouth.

Together, these three methods and the knowledge presented in this chapter will help you access and open your spiritual mouth. This energetic organ is necessary for all of the work we do in this book. The Art of Cosmic Creation cannot be accomplished without opening and engaging the spiritual mouth. The spiritual mouth mirrors the womb of a woman's body. It is a gateway and an entry point where subtle energy can filter down, accumulate, and solidify into physical reality. You have the ability to direct your physical experience of reality through the spiritual mouth. Please note the importance of imagining the wooden nautical wheel in your chest and in your sinus cavity. Because we're reconnecting the subtle to the physical by activating the physical sensations of the spiritual mouth, you must imagine and focus on a physical object. To activate physical sensations, we must first focus on physical, not light, or something intangible to the mind-body machine.

The goal of these exercises is to access and reawaken the spiritual mouth. Once your body reconnects with the sensation, you will be able to activate it at will, like flexing a bicep. You will be able to do it without imagining anything or even breathing deeply. You will turn on the sensations at will and then engage in your desired activity. Once you have mastered opening the spiritual mouth, you can let these exercises go. However, it is still important to access gratitude and joy around you, as we will see later. You can now open the spiritual mouth before and during transforming negative interactions, as outlined in chapter 5. Remember that vibration is felt and not seen. Physical sensations are the link between energy and mass, subtle and physical. The spiritual mouth is the gateway between the two (subtle and physical).

4

The Spiritual Mouth as an Energetic Womb

The Spiritual Mouth mirrors the womb of a woman's body. It is a gateway and an entry point where subtle energy can filter down, accumulate, and solidify into physical reality.

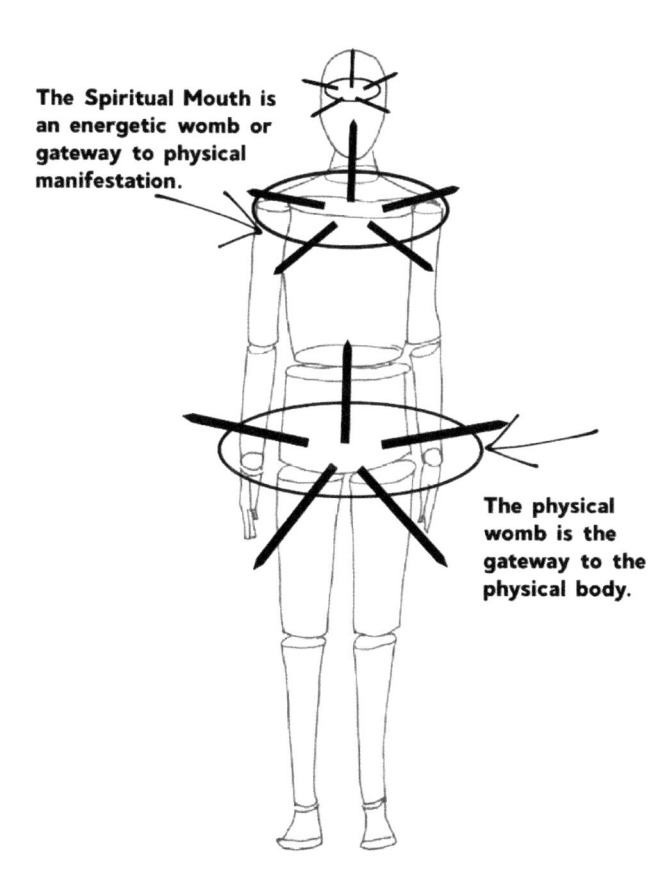

The Spiritual Mouth is an energetic womb or gateway to physical manifestation.

The physical womb is the gateway to the physical body.

125

"Time is an illusion. All exists at once, and all shifts, changes, and develops at once."

~Lavender Moon

7 THE SACRED TRIANGLE OF CREATION
THE PUSH AND PULL OF DESIRE

In real life...

I'm nine years old. I've just woken up suddenly. I heard a noise in my room again for the fifth time in a row. I look at my clock, 3:00 AM, again. I see them, the dim lights I've always seen flying around my room at night. I know they are just my eyes, or what did daddy call it? A hypnagogic hallucination. They aren't real, but I'm still afraid because they look so real. I hear more creaks and noises around me, and my heart begins to pound. I wish I could just sleep the whole night and not wake up. I wish I didn't see these things flying around my room. I reach for my flashlight and turn it on. Suddenly, a thought enters my mind, from out of nowhere, it seems. "Get a pen and paper and start writing."

I reach for my notebook and the pen inside my notebook. I take my blanket and sit on the loveseat by the window. I begin to write a poem rather quickly without thinking. All of the words come to me as if the poem was already written... "The Night" I titled the page.

The night is dark, dismal, and grim.
  There is no light and if there is,
  It's dim.

The night is black and full of shadows that are strange.
Full of figments and pictures,
That always seem to change.

The night is empty and motionless.
Empty of color,
And soundless.

Suddenly, a thought comes into my mind again, "Stop writing now, look out the window." I stop, and I look out the window. There she is, shining brightly in the sky. It must be a full moon tonight. Something seems different, is she shining brighter than usual? Something about her shape, that glowing white orb entrances me. I feel pressure right between my eyebrows and a light fluttering in my chest. Something tells me to finish my poem, so I continue...

The night is sometimes warm and sometimes cold.
Sometimes beautiful,
Once I was told.

If you look hard enough,
You can see that its beauty is true.

I can see it,
How about you?

My body relaxes and somehow I feel better. I climb back into bed and fall asleep.

It is important to become aware of how the energetic world works before we consciously work with it. However, you cannot understand all of it, but we will deliver the necessary parts for your expansion. Before we proceed, let us now integrate our understanding. Just as the chariot requires a direction and reason to move forward, so does your soul require coordinates and the desired destination to move through life. The coordinates on your Guiding Star Compass provide you with the direction/way to reach the required destination/goal. These coordinates give us a reason to change the direction of our lives and a reason to change our paradigms and programming. When we lock into our desired coordinates, energy from our Guiding Self flows into us and radiates outward all around us.

The more in alignment with your Guiding Self your goals are, the easier it is to gain momentum because there is a double energetic force; push and pull, electricity and magnetism, action and attraction. We call this dynamic relationship between the Guiding Self and the partial self, **The Sacred Triangle of Creation**.

As your desire moves closer to you and you closer to your desire, you increase your radiance and your connection to the Guiding Self. As your inner star radiates outward by action and attraction, all areas of your life begin to the line up. By uniting with your Guiding Self through the manifestation of your desires, you experience a sense of wholeness, while still remaining in physical reality. When the partial self unites with that desire by manifesting it, your soul emanates and shines outward from your body, like a reflection from the divine into the physical world.

The Sacred Triangle of Creation

Desire is projected from the Guiding Self and received by the partial self. Conversely, it is the partial self's task to move into action and The Guiding Self's task to facilitate attraction.

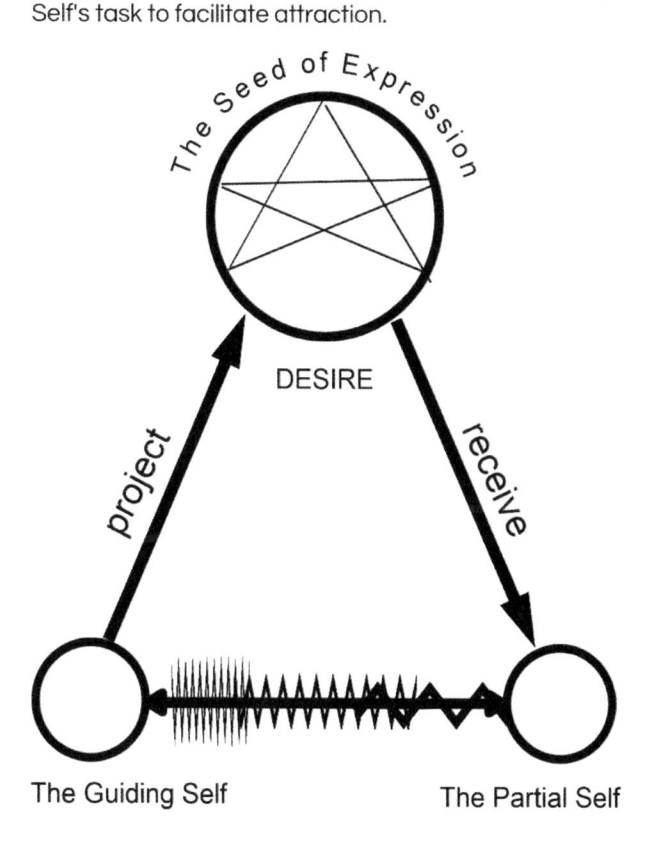

The Seed of Expression

DESIRE

project

receive

The Guiding Self

The Partial Self

Imagine the continuum of duality between the Guiding Self in connection with the Infinite and the partial self, anchored into physical reality. The Guiding Self is vibrating at a higher frequency. Imagine that all of its energy or energetic anatomy (composed of waves) vibrate at the same rate, so there's no differentiation. Its light is white and, therefore, mixed together or united. You and this physical world are differentiated. This differentiation begins in your subtle/energetic anatomy and translates into your physical anatomy.

For example, your hands, feet, and face are all differentiated parts. They are not all mixed together as one unit but exist as separate parts working together. The waves of energy or consciousness are united in the Guiding Self and "slowed down" or "stretched out" to a rate where they begin to differentiate and separate into the partial self, while still being connected to the Guiding Self. The Guiding Self and the partial self are in reality one, as the Guiding Self is one with the Infinite. Separation is only an illusion produced by the "slowing down" and "stretching out" of consciousness. The two are only separated by degree but, in essence, are one in the same.

Energetic Differentiation

Eneretic differentiation or the state of consciousness is reflected through the physical form or mind-body machine.

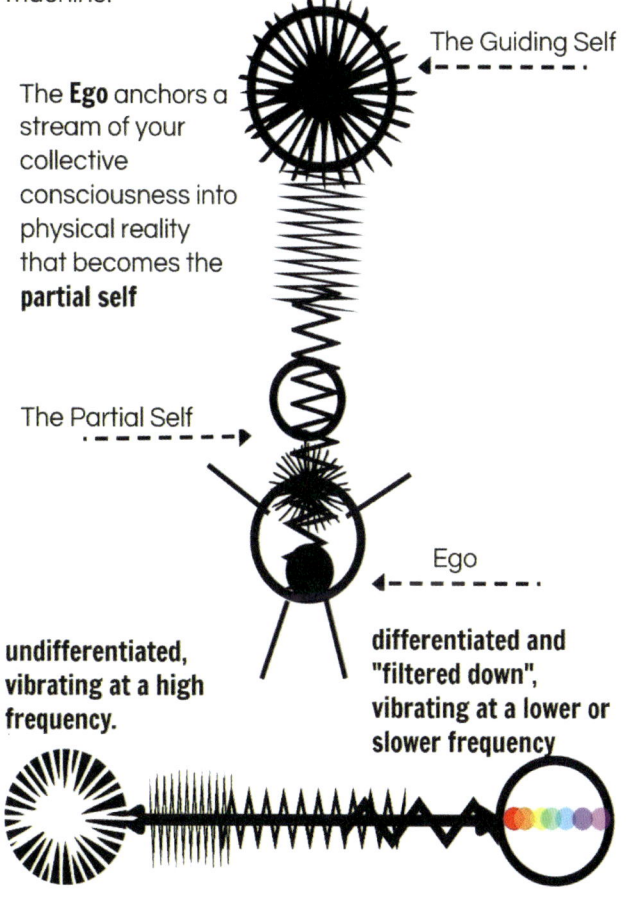

The **Ego** anchors a stream of your collective consciousness into physical reality that becomes the **partial self**

The Guiding Self

The Partial Self

Ego

undifferentiated, vibrating at a high frequency.

differentiated and "filtered down", vibrating at a lower or slower frequency

The Guiding Self

The Partial Self

Now imagine the Guiding Self and the partial self-operating on the horizontal plane. The line represents the continuum of consciousness that connects the two…

The Horizontal Axis

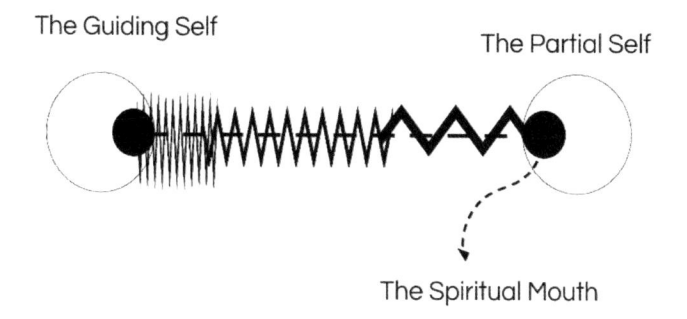

The Guiding Self

The Partial Self

The Spiritual Mouth

The Guiding Self and the partial self are in essence one in the same. The two are only "separated" by their rate of oscillation or rate of frequency.

The horizontal line represents the continuum of consciousness that connects the Guiding Self and the partial self.

The Guiding Self and the partial self intersect at the spiritual mouth. This is the location where desire is received/planted into the partial self.

The horizontal line represents the connection between the TWO (that are in reality, ONE) that is experienced through the spiritual mouth. This is the location through which you can feel the connection. You can imagine the spiritual mouth as a meeting point between your spirit and your soul. The blueprint for your expansion originates in the Guiding Self. This blueprint consists of energetic frequencies that carry information or coordinates for you to follow in physical reality.

These coordinates are necessary due to the disorientation we experience while remaining in this "slowed down" or "stretched out" form of consciousness. This physical reality is disorienting to our consciousness, and for this reason, we are given a blueprint in the form of desire. Desire brings about expansion and expression. Desire is not an Ego-want, which brings about possession and limitation. Desire is the third point in the Sacred Triangle of Creation.

Your blueprints or instructions for expansion and expression originate in the Guiding Self and move through several degrees or dimensions before that desire fixes itself into physical reality. Imagine the movement of a clock where the hand ticks and moves from number to number. In the same way, your blueprints or your desire move from the Guiding Self to you (the partial self) in increments. When the desire finally infuses your being, it emanates or causes your soul to radiate outward into physical reality. This event is like a union with the Infinite. When your desire manifests, your consciousness expands, and as a result, all of creation expands along with you. As your desire moves through the dimensions of reality, the force that "brings it" or "draws it down" into physical reality is the same force that exists in all things physical; the dynamic dance between push and pull, electricity and magnetism, action and attraction. Working together with the Guiding Self in tandem draws the desire into physical reality.

Let us now explain the **5 Stages of Cosmic Creation**...

0° The Real of Ether: The Seed is Formed

At 0°, desire, (your unique blueprints for evolution) is at its place of origin, inside of the Guiding Self. The desire is in its most basic form; it's "seed form" or elemental essence is in the form of vibration, its raw form.

30° The Realm of Air: The Gift of the Seed

At 30°, the seed vibration draws closer to the physical world as it begins to slow down. We refer to this realm as "air" because it is slightly more tangible than ether as your body breathes in the air; this is exactly what happens at 30°. At 30°, you receive the seed vibration through your spiritual mouth. The vibration or package of frequencies/coordinates are amplified and solidified in the resonance chamber. Once in your body, the raw frequency slows down into a "grosser form", like an impregnation. This information rises into the nasal cavity where it is received and interpreted in the brain or conscious mind as a picture.

30° is a receptive state that requires no action on your part. However, to move forward to 90° and continue to solidify, you must be conscious of everything we have told you thus far in this book. This is why most desires end here. You must first reach the level of awakening to "draw your desire down" and fix it into physical reality.

90° The Realm of Water: Tending to the Seed

At 90°, the partial self plants the seed received from the conscious mind by programming it into the mind-body machine via the subconscious mind. Imagine yourself as a farmer here. You have received an important seed. You must prepare the soil, plant the seed, and water it to take root. 90° is the realm of "water" because the package of frequencies that are received by the brain are now solidified further by programming them into the subconscious mind. When we are awakened, we can prepare the subconscious so that the desired coordinates are accepted and programmed into it. These vibrations enter into the cytoplasm of your cells, the cells move into action and your desire takes root in the form of neural-pathways in the brain. As the desire solidifies further into the body, emotional attachments form around the desire.

120° The Realm of Fire: The Heat of Spring

At 120°, the conscious and subconscious minds have been infused by the desire, and the physical body moves into action. The body begins a series of operations known as "habits" that bring the desire into the realm of fire. Transformation occurs here for the soul. This is the stage where your consciousness and awareness grow the most. As the desire moves closer, its intensity and heat are experienced in the form of passion and focus. Just like a star, the intense heat and pressure are what convert subtle elements into gross elements; the same happens here. This stage of development is much like labor, like pushing out the baby, which requires both force and action.

180° The Realm of Earth: Manifestation

At 180°, the desire has taken shape, and fine-tuning occurs as it solidifies into physical reality. Together we have moved from the subtle to the gross. You and your desire are one, and your consciousness expands as a result. All of creation, all awareness has expanded in the expression of your desire. This is giving birth.

The 5 Stages of Cosmic Creation

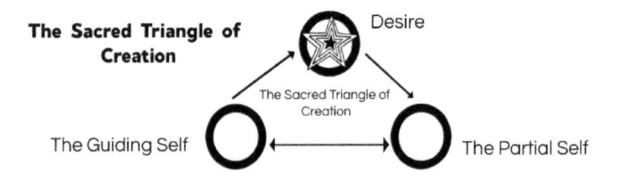

The Sacred Triangle of Creation

Desire

The Sacred Triangle of Creation

The Guiding Self ⟵⟶ The Partial Self

Stage 1 The Realm of Ether: The Seed is Formed

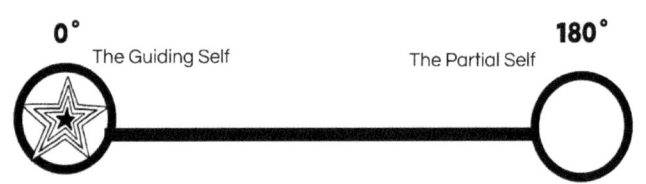

0° The Guiding Self   180° The Partial Self

Desire originates in The Guiding Self on the subtle/energetic side of the continuum.

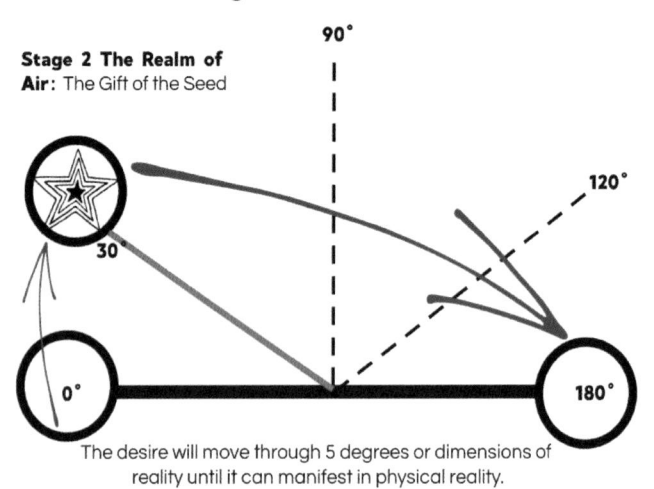

Stage 2 The Realm of Air: The Gift of the Seed

90°
120°
30°
0°   180°

The desire will move through 5 degrees or dimensions of reality until it can manifest in physical reality.

Stage 3 The Realm of Water: Tending to the Seed

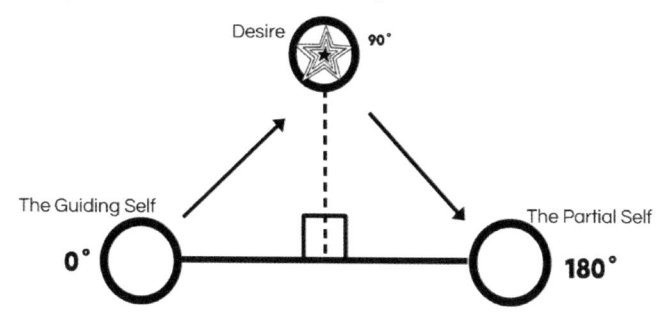

Desire 90°

The Guiding Self 0°

The Partial Self 180°

Stage 4 The Realm of Fire: The Heat of Spring

Desire 120°

The Guiding Self 0°

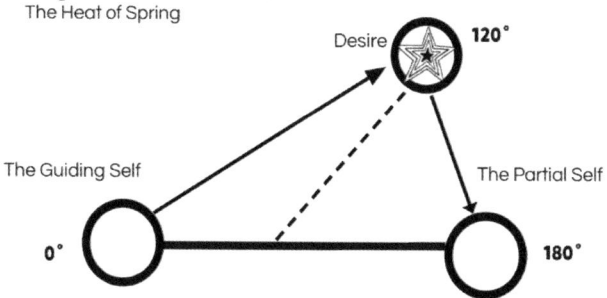

The Partial Self 180°

Stage 5 The Realm of Earth: Manifestation

0° The Guiding Self

The Partial Self 180°

Desire becomes fixed in physical reality and merges with your consciousness causing it to expand and radiate outward.

Throughout each process, we must engage the spiritual mouth. Remember that the spiritual mouth is your connection to the Guiding Self and the energetic world. The spiritual mouth is your organ of resonance. This is where you receive and project frequency to the Guiding Self and into the ether of the Infinite. We will discuss this process at greater length later in the book. It is now important to turn our focus and awareness on the concept of time.

It is helpful to understand that "time" is an illusion. All exists at once, and all shifts, changes, and develops at once. You have now come to understand the concept of "multiple experiences"; that reincarnation is not linear. You are not a separate soul unit that inhabits the physical body for a time and then dies and moves to another. You are a vast consciousness that streams into many mind-body machines at once. All of your lives happen simultaneously as your consciousness explores and experiences multiple perspectives at once. At the same time, your Guiding Self or pool of consciousness continues to exist in another dimension.

When the partial self withdraws from the mind-body machine, that extension of consciousness or rather that tendril of consciousness that extended into the mind-body machine, withdraws back into the Guiding Self. That tendril's song or frequencies are altered and developed through experiencing physical existence. Once this happens, the entire vast consciousness of the Guiding Self is transformed. The Guiding Self sings a new song, as its frequencies have been eternally altered. This evolution affects the entire universe because we are all one consciousness, "separated" by variations of songs. We are like mini branches from one trunk, from one root.

Simultaneous Existence
The Continuum: From Infinite to partial self

The Infinite without Ending

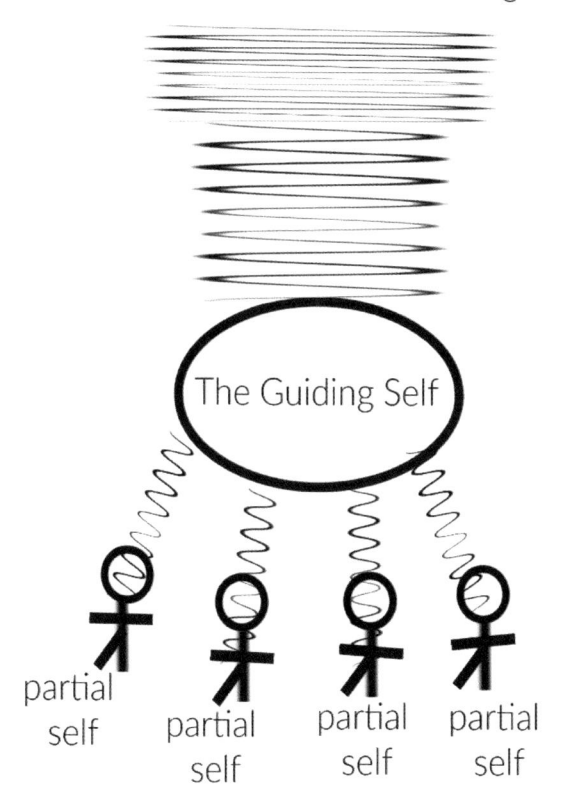

The Guiding Self

partial self   partial self   partial self   partial self

The Guiding Self and the Infinite operate beyond time and space. We only experience time linearly due to our point of view inside the mind-body machine. Our consciousness is "stretched" and "slowed" to the point where we are slightly disoriented. This "stretching" and "slowing of consciousness" affects our perception of time and space. This effect is also a requirement of the soul to carry out and express infinite possibilities. We know or perceive our past and not our future for the same reason. One path, (our past), can visually be seen and remembered while the other path (our future) must be navigated through frequency. This is where the Guiding Star Compass serves as a companion, as it illuminates the darkness.

We don't know the future because we are here to express our potential through a multitude of infinite patterns. The Infinite has created the perfect process to allow creation ITSELF to unfold. We know our past for several reasons. Before birth, we choose the environment and circumstances that will give us the lens/perception or programming that we require. Imagine that your soul wants to create a sculpture, and it will choose ingredients to form just the right type of clay to mold. It will select the base qualities of this clay, like the right color, texture, and density. It is only after this process that the clay can be shaped into a work of art. The formation of the base-clay happens from birth to early childhood as experiences that form the paradigms, which we examined in chapters 3 and 4. These paradigms are reinforced and fine-tuned throughout subsequent years until they become fixed. This is the base clay that you're meant to mold. Your experiences and past paradigms form the soil and fertilizer needed to plant your specific seeds of desire.

To begin to shape, mold, and sculpt the clay that we have chosen as our medium, we must first remember. As we have seen in chapters 3 and 4, it is in the process of remembering that we are able to rise through several levels of awareness and growth, so that we may participate in the Art of Cosmic Creation. Desire is the key to that ascension; it is our soul's blueprint for evolution. The contrast between our first experiences/paradigms and the desire of the Guiding Self is the very thing that creates expansion of awareness and spiritual growth. What we perceive as "the past" is necessary for us to know in order to accomplish the expansion of all creation.

In order to create infinite possibilities and express infinite potentialities, we cannot "know" the future in the same way that we can "know" the past. The past is the clay that we use to sculpt the future. Remember that imagination is the projective part of intuition. This means that you actually do have knowledge of the future because you have the power to see, feel, and experience your desires that have not yet come to pass (or so it seems). They do, however, exist because you CAN see them. This is the tricky part where we become "stuck", and our desires continue to remain in the subtle realms, with potential being unrealized or developed. The seed stays in the earth, never to grow and unfurl its blossom.

It is in getting caught up with "not knowing the future" that the Ego takes over and ensnares you with the limitation of fear and doubt. Needing and wanting to know the future and "certainty", are not connected to the Guiding Self. The illusion of control is connected to the Ego and is a form of "mental grasping". When you engage in "mental grasping", you're caught in the gravitational pull of the Ego's black hole. When we engage and focus on mental grasping, we are moving in the direction of limitation and away from the expansion and expression of our soul. We remain unaware of the future in order to expand our awareness and express the potential of creation. This is the entire point and goal of a physical experience. Time is a tool that we use to accomplish this aim. Release your fears and your mental grasping around the future outcome of your desire with this knowledge. When we look backward, we see with our physical eyes. When we look forwards, we feel with our heart, our spiritual mouth. Understand that these are the two ways we're able to "see". Both are necessary, and both equally as important.

Our spiritual mouth is THE only way to navigate the future that we desire. Release the fears and doubts about accomplishing your desire. The Ego will try to tell you that you need to know every step first, and if you don't, certain disaster will occur. Be aware that the Ego is "limitation". Simply say this to yourself when you find yourself in the Ego's gravitational pull;

"I am aware that you are "limitation", and that is your job. You keep me anchored in this mind-body machine, so that I may participate in The Art of Cosmic Creation. Thank you. This is your job and nothing more. I am aware that I am an expansive being and that my desire is my purpose, my soul's blueprint for evolution, and my path towards expression and expansion."

This message will help you to remember who you are. The Ego is only the glue that keeps you stuck to this body. Remain aware of this.

Having to "know everything" is Ego. Start first by knowing your desire and becoming aware of it. Accept this blueprint as your earthly mission. You will not know or understand how to accomplish most of it, because you are unaware and "not knowing" this is the first step to expanding awareness. Although you are not aware of how to reach that final vision, you are aware of how to begin. The first step is given to you. In the action of taking the first step, you will come to be aware of the second step, third, fourth, etc., until you reach manifestation of that desire. At this point, another level of desire will open up to you, and you will begin the process of Cosmic Creation again, at a faster rate. The first conscious manifestation is the hardest and the longest. After this, you will consciously create at a faster rate. At the time we are writing this book, I (Amber) am not yet aware of how to get this book into your hands. I know how to write with pen and paper, but not how to publish, and yet here you are with this book in your hands. Our desire has been fulfilled, and our creation is expressed.

You have all of the same abilities. You're a vast being with the capability of infinite expression. It is not necessary to know exactly how to get to where you want to go because you have never been there before. Armed with your Guiding Star Compass and with the guidance of the Guiding Self, you'll move in the right direction until your desire becomes fixed in you and birthed into physical reality. However, before any of this can occur, we must first become conscious of our desire.

Exercise 7: **Finding Your Guiding Star**

This exercise can be very tricky because sometimes, what may seem like a desire of the Guiding Self is actually a "want" of the Ego. In other words, the thing that you think is the desire will cause you limitation as it limits your self-expression and internal growth. The path you WANT may have been the desire of another and the road to expansion and expression for THEIR soul, but not YOURS. For this exercise, you must dig deep. You must REMEMBER what you may have long forgotten or taken for granted. The answer may not be straightforward. You may have to pay attention to clues and threads or themes that run throughout your life. *My desire, (Amber), was so subtle and hidden, I almost missed it.*

Please Note: Take your time with this exercise. Examine old photos, family videos, or speak with siblings, cousins, and all who may have played with you as a child (if possible). If you can't remember a stage of your life, move onto the next. Any questions that don't apply, just skip them.

In this exercise, we will use the following questions to excavate your desire if it is hidden, or to fine-tune your desire if you already know it. We will now zero-in on the domain of "service" and examine this domain's development throughout your lifetime.

<u>Early Childhood</u>: Ages 3-6

What did you like to do?
What did you love to pretend to be?
Where did you wish you could be?
How did you like to play?
What did you like to play?
What types of stories or movies or shows were you attracted to?
What did you hate doing?
Is there something that you did naturally that others were impressed with?
How did you enjoy expressing yourself?
When did you feel the most free?
What were you doing then?
What is something that you did that you're proud of?

Childhood: Ages 6-9

Repeat the same questions here and notice any developments or changes. Add on...

What deepened?
What fell away?
Where did you feel the most free and the most self-expressed?
What were you doing that made you feel this free?

Tweens: Ages 10-12

Repeat all previous questions and add on...

Which books were you attracted to?
Which genres did you enjoy?
What came naturally to you?
What were your fantasies and dreams?

Teens: Ages 13-16

Repeat all previous questions and add on...

What did you like to do most when you were away from your friends?
How did you like to express yourself when you were alone?
Who did you want to be like?
What qualities did that person have that you admired?

Young Adult: Ages 17-21

Repeat all previous questions.

Adult: Ages 22-29

Repeat and add on…

What task did you/do you enjoy doing at work?

Adult 2: Ages 30-39

Continue through each decade that applies.

Wherever you end, ask yourself the final set of questions.

What have I forgotten?
What hasn't changed?
What is the common thread of self-expression that runs throughout my life?
What ways of expressing myself feel the most easy and freeing?
In which ways do I force self-expression or development of skills?
Which skills come easy to me?

Spend some time contemplating these questions and answers. To aid in your contemplation we will share a story through Amber's perspective.

I spent most of my life searching for something that I couldn't quite put my finger on. I was always trying to learn new things so that I could find the thing that I felt was lost. I became overwhelmed with the thought, "There's so much to learn; it will take me a million lifetimes to learn it all." I didn't know what I wanted "to be" or to do in this world. I was always plagued by the orbs that I would see at night; too scared to investigate or even talk about them. I could see them best in the dark. I became a teacher because I loved to teach or explain, or break difficult things down until my student understood the concept. That "light of understanding" brought me great joy. However, I always felt like I should be teaching something else, but what? I felt I didn't know enough to teach.

My paranormal experiences have always made me curious and interested in the metaphysical, or was it the other way around? I was always focused on finding the "system" that would be the thing that I could teach, that would bring about something good in this world. Something that could help myself and others, but what? I had this desire to teach and explain something. Since I figured that I had nothing to give, I studied yoga, chakra healing, shamanism, shadow work, and countless other subjects. However, I always felt "fake" or inauthentic when I taught these subjects. I felt limited and confined by these rigid systems. I felt bound by their rules and expectations. A voice inside me said, "You are forcing this because it does not come from you, STOP!"

One day, I listened to that voice, and I stopped everything. I stopped reading the books, stopped teaching yoga, stopped the coaching business that I created, and stopped searching. For once, I listened to that voice inside of my head, and I waited for the next instruction. For a while, I floated in limbo, with no direction, and then it all hit me like a bolt of lightning. I remembered. I remembered everything. I always felt freest when I let the words flow out of me in poetry, writing, and song since I can remember. In all of my earliest childhood memories, I was channeling. I had been channeling all along. It comes easy to me, but I pushed it all away out of fear and doubt.

I pushed it away because of what the world told me. I pushed it all away because I never thought to look within myself for wisdom. All of my searching and studying was only a distraction from the brilliance of my consciousness. I was lost in the darkness of my Ego. Since then, I've discovered the spark inside of me that forever illuminates my way...

We are the same consciousness. You ARE a vast and undeniably expansive being of light. I am here to tell you that this universe is more interesting than we could have previously imagined. You are fully supported and NEVER alone. Take the time to listen to yourself, and you will be amazed by your innate wisdom and potential. You are completely capable of your desires. I always say to myself now, "I can't lose. It's impossible, because these instructions came from my soul, a gift from the Infinite." As you express your potential and expand, so do we all. Never deny creation of your brilliance, never.

What is the one thing that you could do that, in its realization, would bring you the most satisfaction through self-expression? What desire would light up your life, bring you all of the coordinates in your GSC, and project those same feelings into the world around you? What are you naturally able to do that you take for granted? We are meant to serve this world through our natural mode of self-expression. How do you naturally express yourself, and how can you use this mode of self-expression to light up all of creation?

> "Separation is only an illusion produced by the "slowing down" and "stretching out" of consciousness"
>
> ~Lavender Moon

---

8 WITH ACTION COMES ATTRACTION
THE MECHANICS OF HABIT BUILDING

In real life...

I'm three years old. Every night as I lie down in the darkness to fall asleep, I wait to watch the lights as they fly around the room. In the darkness, I see many colors, red, blue, and green. The lines move, and they create all different patterns and shapes. They form what I now understand to be geometric shapes in complex patterns. I used to enjoy watching these lights until I'd naturally drift off to sleep. But this night is different because it's the night when I have to sleep in my own room for the very first time, all by myself.

There! I am tucked into my very own bed with my stuffed Unicorn and Pegasus. My father shuts off the light, and I see them. For the first time as I lay in bed all alone, the lights scare me. It hits me that I don't actually know what they are or why they are flying all around me. I cannot sleep alone with them. I begin to scream, and my parents rush in. I have no name for them. I don't even know what to call them. "The flies! The flies!" I scream. "Turn on the lights! PLEASE! TURN ON THE LIGHTS!" My parents turn on the lights, and I'm hysterical because I don't have the right words. I don't exactly know what THEY are.

My parents explain to me that what I am seeing is not really there. I try to describe the lights, and they tell me that I must have been looking at the light bulb before they shut off the light. I'm so frustrated because I know that they are there, and I know the difference between the light that you see after staring into a light bulb and THEM. I just don't have the right words..." Flies," I keep saying. My father sits with me in the dark until I fall asleep. I still see them, like fireflies leaving a trail of light. As I'm drifting off to sleep in my mind, I hear, "We are They, and They are We."

Over the next few days, this continues. Why do my parents keep bringing me toy bugs and flies to play with? I never did make the connection until I was an adult. They even got me a large toy fly that my mother named "Leisha the fly". Eventually, I learned to ignore the lights. "They are not really there, I just see them," I told myself night after night. Eventually, I forgot about the nights when I would wait in anticipation for their arrival, for the "light show" as I would call it in my mind; all of the pretty colors dancing around, creating beautiful geometry. Over time, I stopped seeing the shapes they created and the colors faded. Now they were only dim lights, easy to ignore, easy to forget. It's amazing the things we can convince ourselves of, and it's amazing what we fear out of the sheer fact that something is unknown to us. I guess I had more to learn from the story of Prometheus than I thought...

The more you immerse yourself into your desire, the stronger your desire for IT becomes. The stronger and more intense your desire becomes, the closer it is to physical reality. The key to intensifying desire and drawing that desire down into physical reality is engaging with your desire constantly. There is no attraction without action and vice versa. Your partial self or the part of you that perceives itself to be YOU is experiencing the physical realm. It exists inside of the mind-body machine, which is built for action. The only way to fix your desire into physical reality is through action. The more you physically engage with your desire, the more your mind-body machine will develop automatic habits that move you into a rhythmic dance with your desire. As this happens, an energetic momentum is created. With every action you take, the world around you invisibly shifts, and energetically rearranges to open the path between you and your desire. This is the Realm of Fire at 120°.

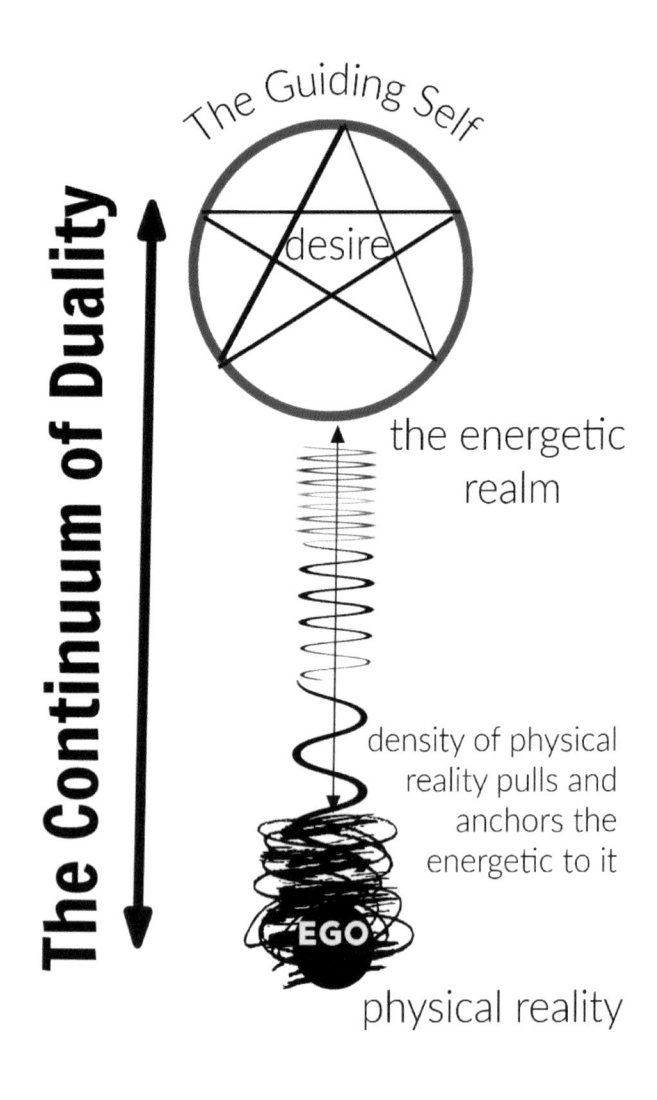

The Continuum of Duality

The Guiding Self

desire

the energetic realm

density of physical reality pulls and anchors the energetic to it

EGO

physical reality

All things move along a continuum of duality. We have presented to you a linear spectrum with two opposite poles; however, it is more like a spiral. All things move in cycles and circular patterns. There is an ebb and flow to all creation. Let us look at the continuum of duality from another perspective, another dimension. Notice the continuum of duality that we already recognize. It appears linear when we look at it from this perspective. But this model does not represent the path or motion our desire takes into physical reality.

Now imagine yourself from the perspective of the desire, looking straight down towards physical reality. In the physical realm, we also move in this way; let us explain. Let us use the same model from our own perspective. Just as the desire moves in a circular pattern, orbiting physical reality, we must draw the desire closer with every revolution until it is close enough to become fixed in physical reality. Physical reality anchors the energetic to it. Once the desire is close enough in orbit, it becomes "caught up" in the gravitational pull of physical mass and unites with it, just as our consciousness unites with our temporary mind-body machine.

Your actions draw the desire closer to you, and in turn, consciously programmed habits move you in an orbit around your desire. Every revolution or repetition of your habit moves you closer to the manifestation of your desire at 180°. It is not just the goal of your desire that is important, but to truly manifest, repetition is needed, and repetition is exactly what the mind-body machine is designed to do. In addition to habits or repetitious actions setting you into orbit, the mind-body machine works in cycles of energetic flow.

The Orbit of Action and Attraction

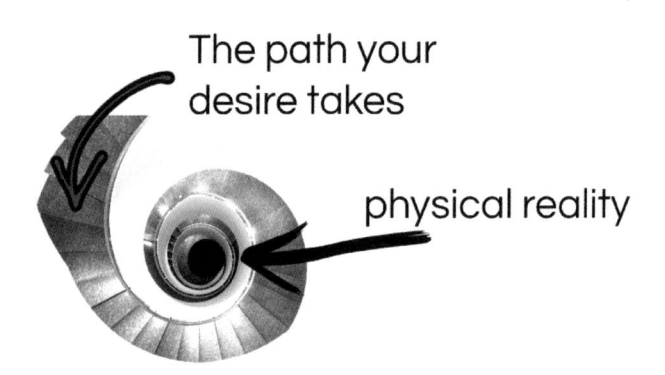

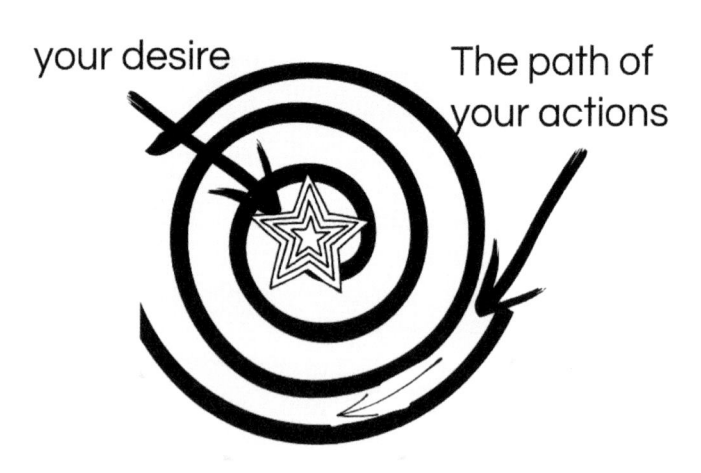

The path your desire takes

physical reality

your desire

The path of your actions

Each body can be different, so there is no set rule for every BODY. We all have personal cycles of energetic timing. Some of us are more active and connected early in the day and others at night. Form your habits around your natural energy patterns. Let us now review and explain how to program habits into the mind-body machine.

The mind-body machine is exactly what we call it, a machine. It's a vehicle that you-as-consciousness operate, to exist in physical reality and operate within the "laws" of this dimension. Remember that you are not your mind or your body. Your Ego is the "glue" that fixes your consciousness to this mind-body machine. You-as-consciousness are the driver of this machine, and YOU, therefore, have the power of choice in how to make it move and act. It's as easy as this: Once you become aware of how to operate your vehicle, just like a car or bicycle, you begin to operate with ease.

The mind-body machine was designed for repetition because it is this daily repetition of motion, tuned to your coordinates, that draws your desire down to you and fixes it into physical reality. With every habitual repetition of action, your desire makes one revolution and draws closer. Being aware of this is the key to understanding The Art of Cosmic Creation. All things move in cycles, orbits, spirals, and repetition. In order to install a program for a particular habit, we must first condition the mind consciously, to support these habits. The "treatments" that we have given you are designed to attune your mind to the Guiding Self. Your treatments serve as a primer or a strong foundation on which you can build.

After you have your treatments in order and are repeating them or listening to them daily for two to three weeks, you are ready to construct the program that you need to draw your desire down to you. Before we give you the exact process, it is helpful to see a specific example. For this example, we will speak through the perspective of Amber…

I had a deep desire to write this book, but I couldn't seem to get started because I had no time. I woke up at 5 am every morning so that I could get ready for work. I had a full day at work, and then I returned home around 5:00 pm, exhausted from my day. My family also required my attention and care. Before I knew it, it was bedtime. How would I ever get my writing done? Lavender Moon answered me. The process that I was about to go through was crucial for the book, as you are about to understand. "She" answered, "Do what comes easy to you."

The first thing I had to become conscious of were my requirements for the task. I needed to be alone in order to channel. I had to be comfortable, safe, and I needed total silence, and most importantly, no interruptions. The second thing Lavender Moon asked me to become aware of was my "personal cycle of energy". I am most awake and most focused and intuitive in the morning. After work, I am tired and don't like mental activities. I am also distracted and needed by my family. "You will wake up at 4:00 am to write," said Lavender Moon. 4:00 am met all of my requirements and my personal cycle of energy. I felt resistance, however.

I began thinking of waking up at 4:00 am and how early it was. I began worrying that it would make me too tired and that the rest of my day would be difficult because of my energy level. Lavender Moon reminded me that I was "grasping" with my mind and that I felt resistance because I "missed a step". I had forgotten to condition my mind first before I could act on the habit I desired to create. I recorded several affirmations that included the habit that I wanted to adopt and the feelings that they would bring. I said something like,

"I wake up every morning at 4:00 am to write my book with energy. Writing my book makes me feel connected, awake, alive, and joyful."

As soon as I woke up in the morning, I would put on my headphones and listen. At night just before bed, I would listen again until my mind began to drift.

As I would listen, something interesting would happen. I would start to mentally grasp, and I would think thoughts like, "I don't want to get out of bed that early, I want to sleep." Lavender Moon helped me notice how many times I said, "want", and I realized that it was my Ego doing its job of "limitation". I relaxed and breathed as I said, "Ok, Ego. I'm not waking up at 4:00 am, I'm just relaxing and listening to this recording. All I have to do is listen and relax. I'm doing everything I need to do. Just listen." I would relax, repeating this every time my Ego chimed in. I realized my mental grasping quicker and quicker each time. Very soon, the voice of resistance was quiet.

After around two to three weeks of listening to my affirmations, I naturally woke up at 4:00 am one day. I decided to get up and write. The words flowed out of me, and I felt amazing. That night, I listened to my affirmations again. This time I set my alarm for 4:00 am, and when I woke up, I felt excited to start writing. Over time, as I began to write constantly for two weeks, I stopped listening to my affirmations because I now embodied the habit. Every word that you are reading was written at 4:00 am. I began to look forward to my writing time so much that on days where I couldn't wake up at 4:00 am, I felt "off", and *couldn't wait for my next writing session. You hold the result of my habit in your hands as a manifestation of my desire.*

Now that you have YOUR desire in mind, we can begin to design the habits that will call your desire "down" and fix it into physical reality. Every repetitive motion shapes the clay into the structure that you desire. There are several things to be considered when forming a habit in addition to the time of day. Consistency and repetition are the keys to Cosmic Creation. With each repetitive motion, the clay is shaped into the structure that you desire. Habits have to work with your life; they must work within your personal cycles of energy and slowly shift your current reality. To do this, they must fit into your current reality. Scheduling is key in the beginning. Understand that we are giving you exact structures to begin the process. You will no longer require most of these structures after some time. Let us shift back to the perspective of Amber to explain.

I now understand that 4:00 am was the perfect time to complete things that require no disruption. I had two habits that I wanted to put into action. I wanted to write so that I could publish this book, and I wanted to feel healthier and stronger. I wanted to exercise for 30 minutes a day, but my son would interrupt me if I did it in the afternoon (as three-year-olds do!), and on top of that, I was physically tired. All I wanted to do was lay down on the couch under the blanket and watch a show. My whole life, I had showered and relaxed after work. I realized that I needed to work within this structure in order to make things sustainable for myself. I needed to enjoy my time.

I decided that my new habit would be to wake up at 4:00 am. Monday, Wednesday, and Friday, I would write. Tuesday, Thursday, and Saturday (at 6:00 or 7:00 am), I would exercise. This meant that when I came home, I could rest and relax with my family. I had other desires, like a clean home. I created a habit to wipe-down the bathroom while my son took a bath. I had to be in there anyway, so why not clean up at the same time? Over time, I created more habits, one or two for each domain of physical reality like walking with my husband on Sundays, calling extended family members on Fridays, prepping my food for the week on Sundays. I started reading bedtime stories to my son Mondays, Wednesdays, and Fridays, while my husband did the other days and so on. Pretty soon, I had routines that worked with my energy levels, and every day I did these things automatically. Lavender Moon taught me that the most important thing is repetitive motion. So if that day I messed up, or didn't get to do something because something else came up, I let go and continued with my routine the next day. If something wasn't working, or if I felt resistance, I changed or modified it, and I kept moving.

Resistance is a very good type of feedback. Resistance means that you are going against your natural flow or cycle of personal energy. It can also mean that you have missed a step. The perspective of Amber is helpful here.

When I first began to write this book, I picked up my laptop, and I began to type. I hated this. I didn't feel the flow and the connection that I felt when I channeled. The whole task felt tedious and impossible. I was experiencing resistance. I closed my laptop and waited for guidance. I received the message that I had missed a step. I needed to type the book in order for it to be published, but first, I needed to WRITE IT. Ah, that's it, I missed a step. I picked up my pen, a blank notebook, and the book itself began to flow out of me as if this book was writing itself. I just had to find a way of writing the book that came naturally to me, and that was with a pen and paper. It's the way that I've always channeled.

Another example of working with my natural energy was when I chose my exercise routine. "Yoga is what I should be doing if I'm enlightened, right? Running and yoga are the best. Vinyasa flow looks cool". The problem was that I had resistance to these forms of exercise. I learned not to force myself but to find instead, an exercise that works with my energy. I'm naturally slow and methodical in everything that I do. Walking and slow weight lifting suited me nicely, and because I enjoy it so much, I rarely miss a session. Always look at what pace, skill, and time come naturally to you. Those things are in place for a reason.

When forming new habits, we must be mindful of the way we vibrate naturally. Everything must be tailored to your desires and not the other way around. Be aware that you are the sovereign who sits at the center of your five domains of self-expression. These domains are yours by divine right. It is your purpose to mold and shape each domain into the likeness of your desire; into your unique strand of consciousness. The path of action is the path to your desire. Allow your motions to be aligned with your unique cosmos, and you will never fail.

Exercise 8: 120° Creating a System of Action

Step 1: Take some time to review your GSC, your unique vision for each domain, and the coordinates that you wish to experience.

Step 2: For each domain, decide on a simple action that you could repeat at the same time and day, or days of each week, that would make the most difference or accomplish the most in that domain. Choose ONLY one action for each domain. It is important to build habits slowly and one at a time, or the habit will fail.

Step 3: Consider your current schedule, cycles of energy, and personal preferences when selecting a day, time, and duration.

Step 4: Write a set of affirmations for each domain that include your vision or goal for that domain, how it will feel, and what you will do ALL in the present tense.

>Use sentences like
>I am _____
>I have_____.
>I feel so (positive feeling) when I (desired habit).

>For example: I desire a beautiful, fit body, and so I write these affirmations...
>I am beautiful.
>I have a strong, healthy, and toned body.
>I feel so alive when I exercise.

>I use the above to create this extended affirmation...

I have a lean, beautiful, and healthy body. I am confident, energetic, and radiant. I wake up every day at 4:00 am to start my day with energy and movement. It feels so good to move. Exercise makes me feel ALIVE and POWERFUL.

Step 5: Record your affirmations and listen to them daily when you wake up and when you're falling asleep at night. Adding beautiful music enhances the effect of these affirmations. If you feel resistance, just release mental grasping by reminding yourself that all you have to do is listen. You don't need to do anything but listen. Don't begin action until your desire becomes strong to begin.

Step 6: Begin action. Open your spiritual mouth when beginning these actions. If something doesn't feel right or if it's hard to maintain, then you may have missed a step. Readjust, recalibrate, or try something else, but keep moving.

As you work with your habits, it is important to only try to implement ONE at a time, or a maximum of two. Wait until you've been doing the habit consistently for three weeks until you try another. Little by little, your surroundings will begin to shift, and you will be amazed at the synchronicities that your actions begin to attract to you.

> "All things move in cycles and circular patterns. There is an ebb and flow to all creation"
>
> ~Lavender Moon

9 THE ART OF COSMIC CREATION
PUTTING IT ALL TOGETHER

In real life...

I am 38 years old. My brother and I have just arrived at the historic Morris Jumel Mansion in New York City. It's 9:00 pm, and the moon is full, a perfect evening for a paranormal investigation. This was a birthday gift from me to my brother. I booked a private paranormal investigation where we would learn about the history of the mansion and try out some of the tour guide's equipment. I didn't expect anything out of the ordinary to happen. I had never been on a paranormal investigation before and having no equipment myself, I only brought a digital camera.

As we sat in chairs in the main entrance and listened to our guides introduce themselves, and talk about the history of the mansion, I suddenly see movement in my periphery. It's nothing special because I see these things all the time, and I'm so used to ignoring them, that it happens automatically. "It's not real. It's just my eye," is the thought that flickers through my mind. We go upstairs, and in the darkness, I see faint balls of light moving here and there— nothing I haven't seen before.

Our guides place a motion sensor on the bed. As we leave the room, it begins to light up. We enter the room again, and I see a faint ball of light dart around the room. The hair begins to stand up on my arms. "Could it be?" I see the ball of light float over the bed again, and the sensor goes off. I instinctively lift up my camera and take a picture. There it is, a perfectly round sphere of light hovering directly over the sensor. I spend the rest of the night taking pictures every time I see the balls of light, and I come home with more than 20 photos of orbs. "If I can take a picture of it, then how can it be my eye???"

My whole life, I am usually awakened at around 3:00 am, and directly above my face, I can see an orb of light. Every night I turn around and go back to sleep. Tonight, I keep my camera next to my bed. I wake up, and there it is! I sit up and snap a picture. There are four balls of light surrounding my bed. I begin crying, not out of fear but out of deep sadness and frustration. "All this time, what I was seeing was true. It's real. All this time, I doubted myself and didn't trust my own eyes." Then a thought drifted into my head almost of its own accord, "The veil has been lifted. You are aware, and you are ready." "Ready for what?" I whisper into the darkness...

The Art of Cosmic Creation can be summed up in the lines of the Disney theme song that was cited at the beginning of this book.

"When you wish upon a star, makes no difference who you are."

Your "wish" is the focus that you apply to your desire. You focus in the direction of the "star" or your desire, because it seeks its potential expression through you. On the continuum, your desire is the seed of possibility. Your desire, or "star", contains the seeds of consciousness desiring expression. At the same time, your spirit seeks to develop and cultivate these seeds of consciousness to express its greatest potential.

It is the merging of your spirit and the desire of the Guiding Self, that produces a radiance that illuminates all of creation with awareness. Our unique perceptions, based on our life experiences, produce the infinite filters needed to produce infinite possibilities. All of us, no matter who we are or rather who we appear to be, are a vital part of this cosmic symphony. Without "you", all could not exist. Stay aware and remember this when you become disoriented due to physical existence. You are a vast consciousness that surpasses the limits of time and space. Remind yourself by saying:

"Through me, I give form to the formless. This is called Cosmic Creation, for we are all stars forming matter out of nothingness, tangible from intangible."

"Anything your heart desires, will come to you."

Maintain awareness of your connection to the Guiding Self. Open the spiritual-energetic mouth; this is your pathway for communication with all vibration. Together with the focus of your mind, drink into yourself, the desired feelings of your Guiding Star Compass. Draw your desire down to you so that the coordinates merge with your energetic system. Over time, your frequency will begin to match and operate as one. Be aware of your ability to call your desire into the present, and into your presence from the ether, and into your physical reality. Allow the action of movements and cycles to serve as a beacon that attracts your desire to you with every revolution.

Imagine your reality, your five domains of self-expression, as a garden. For this practice, focus on one desire at a time. Before planting the seed, you must make sure that the ground is fertile and can support the growth of this seed. Use your treatments to prepare your subconscious to accept and nurture your desire. The treatments are the nutrients and minerals that your desire requires. The soil is your life, your unique experience created by merging and anchoring Ego with your consciousness. Remember that you exist along a continuum, in order to operate within physical reality.

The Ego serves its purpose of limitation. Do not identify with it; remember its function and your true identity. All that you see in your life is a mirage. Your surroundings are the result of creation without awareness. Ghosts that are echoes of the past may roam your surroundings. Fear, doubt, guilt, anger, and sadness are the weeds that threaten your garden. They are agents of the Ego that will drain your seed before it can sprout. Release mental grasping, be aware of your ghosts, and then choose your focus. Your focus acts as the shears that will remove the weeds from your garden. Focus on your desire; do not identify with the ghosts or echoes of the past. As your desire develops and gains momentum, the old vibrations will disintegrate back into the ether. All creation exists along this continuum.

Next, your garden requires water to stimulate and nourish your seed. You must tend to your garden daily to remove weeds with focus, and water the seeds by drinking their coordinates or instructions for expression through your spiritual mouth. This is true prayer and true gratitude. As you focus on the image of your desire, open the spiritual mouth, and with every inhalation, feel yourself, drinking the feelings of that vision into your energetic system.

Imagine your seed within your chest. The more you drink and breathe the vision into your body, the quicker this seed will grow.

Release mental grasping and the deception of control. Your Guiding Self directs your awareness to your next step when you are ready. The more you release grasping, the more you open to the wisdom of the Guiding Self. Look for evidence of your desired coordinates in the sunshine, in the smile of a loved one, in the warm water. Become aware of your desired coordinates, as they exist in your current domains. Drink the moment into your spiritual mouth until you become saturated with them. Awareness is true gratitude; your awareness brings a light that attracts and accumulates these coordinates to you. They feed and bring growth to your desire. Tend to your garden daily.

Align your actions to the desire of the Guiding Self. Program the mind-body machine to move in revolutions around your desire. As you act in repetition, you increase the density of your desire. As that density increases, so does its gravitational pull. All that is in alignment with that desire is pulled towards it. With action comes attraction. Work with the core of who you are in this lifetime and not against it. Your life is the clay that you chose to shape. The growth and success of your garden depend upon the synergy of nature and physical labor. Each side requires the other, and desire cannot come to fruition without both forces working in tandem according to that desire.

Finally, your garden requires sunlight to grow and prosper—the light of awareness triumphs over the darkness of fear. Bring awareness to every motion and revolution of action. Remember in every moment who you are. Use your spiritual mouth to drink in the awareness that with every repetitive movement, your desire moves closer along the continuum of duality. Drink in the light of that knowledge as you act, as you focus, as you look, and as you feel. Remember that vibration is consciousness and that you have the power to direct and accumulate consciousness based on your awareness. Your focus determines your direction along the spectrum of duality.

You are a vast pool of consciousness existing in multiple realities at once. We are all connected like roots that intertwine underground. When you live a life fully expressed, when you radiate your desire through the five domains of physical reality, your awareness brings light to all consciousness. Your creation brings potential into expression, and we all expand as a result. All of creation desires your expansion and radiance. All of creation waits for your light to shine with infinite anticipation. You reflect and express the Infinite through your very existence. You are the ruler and sovereign of your domains by divine right. Remember who you are, and the lamp of awareness will guide you through even the darkest night.

Exercise 9: A Recipe for Cosmic Creation

It's important to note that the most important act is to maintain awareness of WHO and WHAT you really are. You are already a master of the Art of Cosmic Creation. This is a process that actually comes naturally to you. Once you accomplish and express one desire, you will be able to manifest all future desires with increased momentum and ease. The first time is always the most challenging, but once you remember, you can never forget.

Step 1: Choose your Destination

Work through the chapters to fill out your Guiding Star Compass. Let this compass serve as an infographic that contains within it, a tangible blueprint that will guide you in your journey through the Art of Cosmic Creation. The Guiding Star Compass is a metaphor or symbol for the vibrational seed that you receive from your Guiding Self. The GSC is here to remind you that you DO know the way and that you possess all that you need to navigate. Here you will identify your:

· Five coordinates;
· Grand vision for self-expression (your purpose);
· Your first goal, desire to bring to fruition; and,
· Your ideal expression of each domain (look at this daily as you continue the next steps.

Step 2: Recondition the Subconscious

Play your treatments when the conscious mind releases its grasp and the gateway to the subconscious is open; when you lie down to sleep and when you rise up in the morning, when you are drifting into sleep and when you are drifting back into consciousness. Allow this process to continue for two or three weeks until you feel a positive shift in your awareness. Your dreams will be a good indication of this shift. Your subconscious mind will playback more personal power through your dreams.

Step 3: Shift your Focus

Carry out this step simultaneously with step two. Begin to focus on the expression of your coordinates already present within your domains. For example, if one of your coordinates is "beauty", focus on something in your life that radiates beauty, a flower, a song, even a piece of clothing in an advertisement. Instead of focusing on possession or lack of attainment, focus on its beauty, and open the spiritual mouth. In appreciation, drink the beauty into you with each breath. Do this with all of your coordinates. Anything can be appreciated: laughter, the sound of birds, a taste, a touch. Synchronicities will begin to happen, drink these in as well.

Step 4: Accessing your Vision

Begin to imagine a clear picture of the attainment of your desire. Repeat to yourself in the present tense, the attainment of this desire, "I am the author of the book The Art of Cosmic Creation". Feel your soul radiating outward in the attainment of that goal and open the spiritual mouth as you drink in the power of expression. Do this once per day when you are by yourself on the train, in the shower, etc. There is no time limit on this exercise: 5, 10, or 30 minutes do not make a difference. It is consistency and frequency that counts.

Step 5: Step into Action

After two to three weeks of steps 1-4, decide on your habits and when/how often they are to be repeated. Record the habits and positive feelings to be installed. Choose routines that will facilitate the frequency and consistency of these actions. Add one at a time. Listen to this recording for two weeks and then implement the habit; fine-tune as needed. Open the spiritual mouth and drink in the coordinates as you listen to your recording, and as you carry out the action. Drink in the accomplishment of its completion for that day.

Step 6: The Light of Awareness Expands

While in step 5, remember to drink in all synchronicities, new ideas, and expressions of your coordinates every day. Notice shifts in your domains and acknowledge these shifts by drinking them in. Every time you drink, you add density to your desire. With action comes attraction; with attraction comes action.

Step 7: The Supernova Effect – Manifestation

It is very important to keep the details of your goal as secret as possible. For example, I told everyone that I was writing a book, but I did not share the book's contents or information. This creates a container within you where the desire for manifestation builds up. This increase in energy builds the pressure needed to transform subtle into gross, just like a star. Everything you do is designed to increase the heat and pressure of your desire so that it has the transformative energy to burst into existence. Once you have manifested your desire, drink it into you and radiate with the knowledge and awareness you have gained through its manifestation.

> "Out of awareness flows all possibilities"
>
> ~Lavender Moon

10 A VISION FOR THE FUTURE
TRANSITION THROUGH THE AGES

Just as we have a spiritual mouth, so does the earth herself. We are all part of the same pool of consciousness. The tree of life is the tree of earth. The magnetic core is the spiritual mouth of earth, which can be accessed through the poles. The earth moves and aims herself at the stars. These groups of stars or constellations produce a frequency that represents the collective desire of the earth's consciousness. These movements and synchronization/communication between earth and stars are the "ages"; moving from Virgo, to Leo, to Cancer, to Gemini, to Taurus, to Aries, to Pisces, and now to Aquarius.

The magnetic pole focuses on that particular frequency, and those coordinates are pulled down into earth's consciousness through the spiritual mouth. This desire is solidified through all consciousness existing in the physical reality on earth. This desire is solidified and expressed through all beings, from the microscopic, through the minerals, through the plants, through the animals, and through humanity itself.

Humanity, therefore, is in a transition, and so, your collective consciousness is shifting. Language is limiting. True language, or universal language, is frequency that produces a shape, which you call geometry. This geometry creates a certain order; frequency orders the "ether" around us. When old energy or frequency begins to transition, like all things in this physical realm, it must fall apart or break down. Remember, there is always a balance in physical reality. One structure must disintegrate in order to make room for another.

During this transition, the old vessel, the old order, or organization of ether will begin to melt, break down, and liquefy into its original substance. As this transition occurs, the old structure will become agitated, unstable, and reactive. The dying structure will try and hold on because this is the Ego's natural inclination. The Ego is there to anchor the structure in physical reality through limitation. The Ego tries to stop the old structure from liquefying and melting back into the Infinite, but the glue is only temporary. As a result of this Ego-agitation, the structure becomes erratic and violent before it's end. Remaining aware of this process and connecting with the eternal Guiding Self will lead you safely to the other side during this transition.

The time of Aquarius, it's song, it's frequency, and it's structure, calls us into a new level of awareness and a new level of connection with the Divine. Humanity will slowly turn from worshipping idols. We define an idol as anything outside of yourself. This song calls you to look within yourself, to connect to the Infinite inside of you by co-creating with the Guiding Self on an individual level as well as from a higher perspective.

The Guiding Self is one with the Guiding Self of earth consciousness. Your spiritual mouth is one with the spiritual mouth of the heavenly earth-body. Your self-expression, growth, and expansion are one with the vision of earth herself. Science and spirituality, humanity, and nature will become one. Just as you reflect and express the Infinite, so do your creations reflect and express your current state of consciousness. As you grow and evolve, so do your desires and your creations. Creations and desires will begin to shift along the continuum of duality. During this era, creations will move away from the limitation of the Ego and towards the expansion of the Guiding Self. The future of humanity and the future of the cosmos depend upon you being able to grasp this concept.

Over the next 2,000 years, these changes will occur. As we move into this new level of awareness, (which has already begun), the world will begin to re-order itself around you. As your consciousness ascends, you begin to operate at a higher/faster-moving frequency. As a result, you will be "closer" to the energetic-subtle realms than you were before. This "closeness" creates a transparency in the "veil" that separates or creates the distinction between the physical and the energetic. This "merge" has already begun as well, and you will experience more intersection of the two dimensions as time goes on.

Amber has asked the questions: "Why do you come to us now? Why do you communicate with us at all?" This has been the age-old dance since before our time. In our infancy, others assisted us, and others assisted them. This is the way it has always been because of the understanding of the nature of consciousness and the process of expansion. Every so often, there are great cataclysms in every world. This guidance allows for steady growth even after these cataclysms. It is our continual desire to assist in the expansion of all consciousness because, at our current state, we can feel the connection between us and all beings throughout the cosmos (of which there are many).

We have been with you (humanity), since your inception and even before your entrance into the physical. We have made humanity aware of many different concepts throughout time. We do not only communicate through one person and one book, but through many. Every transition into another age requires a re-write or an update as older writings and messages become misinterpreted, and as humanity shifts its awareness. We come to you now with the desire of awareness because from awareness flows all possibilities. We are here to bring awareness to all of the concepts that we have presented in this book. It is up to you to choose your direction along the continuum of duality. Understand yourself, and you will understand all of creation.

"When you wish upon a star,

Makes no difference who you are.

Anything your heart desires,

Will come to you..."

~Leigh Harline & Ned Washington for Walt Disney's 1940 adaptation of Pinocchio

ABOUT THE AUTHOR

Amber Tawn's mission is to empower others to trust their authentic selves and follow their intuition. She is a natural communicator and communicates with a collective consciousness she calls Lavender Moon.

Through Lavender Moon, Amber channels messages that help people expand their awareness, connect with what brings them joy, and do what's necessary to shape their lives into an expression of their true spirit.

Amber's YouTube channel of the same name, "Lavender Moon" is where she teaches tarot as a tool to develop intuition and self-trust and shares the messages of Lavender Moon. When she's not writing and helping others, she enjoys connecting with Mother Nature in the great outdoors, walks on the beach, orb photography, and spending as much time as she can with her husband, son, and their little havapoo, Saffie.

To learn more about Amber, visit www.ambertawn.com

Printed in Great Britain
by Amazon